Radical Jesus

The heart of radical discipleship

John Vincent

All proceeds from the sale of this book are used for the work of the Urban Theology Unit and the Sheffield Inner City Ecumenical Mission.

Marshall Pickering

Marshall Morgan and Scott
Marshall Pickering
3 Beggarwood Lane, Basingstoke, Hants RG23 7LP, UK

First published in 1986 by Marshall Morgan and Scott
Publications Ltd
Part of the Marshall Pickering Holdings Group
A subsidiary of the Zondervan Corporation

ISBN: 0 551 01344 3

Phototypeset in Linotron Plantin and Rockwell
by Input Typsetting Ltd, London
Printed in Great Britain by
Anchor Brendon Ltd, Tiptree, Essex.

Contents

5

Preface

Since 1970, I have lived and worked in the inner city of Sheffield. Before that, I worked in Manchester and Rochdale. In my twenties, I spent several years, studying the Gospels – in London, in the USA, and in Basel, Switzerland. I have been studying and writing about the Gospels, especially Mark, ever since. But I have almost learnt as much about the Gospel stories from working in the urban wilderness of today as I have from studying all the books about the New Testament.

Especially, I have learnt new ways of understanding Jesus from colleagues and participants in the Urban Theology Unit. Here, every year, people of all ages and backgrounds come to reformulate their theology and their vocation, in the light of the contemporary implications of the way of Jesus.

So that, as I tell the story of Jesus in Mark's Gospel, I shall also tell how it makes sense of and interprets, challenges and supports things which I experience happening today. And that story is as radical in our world today as it was when Jesus first acted it out.

Jesus the radical walks my streets, creates my communities, freaks out my neighbours, judges my friends, calls my enemies, offends my fellow ministers, heals my sick neighbours, breaks into my world views, exposes my betrayals. He does it now, just as he does it in the Gospel story.

But before you believe that, you'll need to hear the story of radical Jesus as the first disciples encountered it and wrote it down. That is what this book is about.

Then, I hope, when you have read it, you'll think with me that there's nothing more worth doing in life than being a disciple of that same radical Jesus today.

A number of members of the Community around here have helped with this book. Twelve months ago, Chris Bruce, Frances Dales, Richard Levitt, Moira Neish and I worked together on the *Radical Jesus Manifesto* used in the first Radical Jesus Campaign in May. I have adapted some of my bits in the *Manifesto* for this volume. I am also very grateful to Pat Hamilton, Mark Woodhead and Grace Vincent for doing the typing and to Grace and Margaret Mackley for work on the proofs.

JOHN J. VINCENT
Urban Theology Unit,
210 Abbeyfield Road,
Sheffield S4 7AZ

January 1986

Note on Gospel Translations

All references in brackets are to the Gospel of Mark. Thus 5.2 means Mark chapter 5 verse 2. When other gospels are referred to, this is indicated (Mt = Matthew, Lk = Luke, Jn = John).

As the New Testament was written in Greek, it is hard to give an exact translation, and if one knows the Greek, no modern translation ever pleases always. So the translation is the author's, and sometimes I translate the same passage differently in different contexts, to try to give the feel of the original.

It will help readers if they have a copy of Mark's Gospel beside them, to follow references. There is an excellent small edition of Mark's Gospel in the Good News Bible version, published by the Bible Society at 25p. The best versions, in my view, are the New Jerusalem Bible (Darton Longman and Todd, 1985) and the American Revised Standard Version (Nelson, 1979). The Good News Bible for Modern Man (Fontana, 1980) is excellent and very readable, but occasionally gets things wrong, as does the New English Bible (Oxford & Cambridge, 1970). But any of these four are good – or more than one, if possible, to compare their translations.

Also, I often use the 'dramatic present tense', as Mark sometimes does. Though he wrote in AD 66–70 to people far away from Galilee of AD 30–33, Mark wanted to say, 'The story is still going on'. I want to say the same. And I do not differentiate what Mark wrote from what early stories handed on, or from what actually happened. I take Mark as it stands.

Part One: Radical Jesus

He left, and went back to his own home town, with his disciples following him.

When the Sabbath day came, he commenced teaching in the synagogue. There was a large congregation which heard him, and they were all full of wonder.

'Where does he get all this from?', they asked.

'What wisdom is this that has been given to him?'

'How does he work such miracles? Surely, this is only the carpenter, Mary's son, the brother of James, Joseph, Judas and Simon! And aren't those his sisters here with us?'

So they fell foul of him.

Mark 6. 1–3

1: Northerner

Jesus was a Northerner.

Palestine was divided into several separate areas. Jesus came from Galilee, the northern province of Israel. Galilee was an island of Judaism surrounded by Gentile, non-Jewish areas. To the north and west were the international trading ports of Tyre and Sidon, Syro-Phoenician areas. To the east were heathen areas and the Roman 'ten towns' (Decapolis). To the south, Greek Scythopolis and Samaritan Samaria separated Galilee from Judea and Jerusalem, the home of 'real' Judaism.

The name 'Galilee' was derived from the area being called 'the District (*Gelil*) of the Gentiles', as Isaiah 9.1 makes clear. From 4 BC to 39 AD, Galilee was administered by a 'Tetrarch' of the house of Herod, called Antipas. Taxes were paid to him, not to Rome. Heads of synagogues like Jairus (Mk.5.22) were also chief local officials on behalf of the Tetrarch.

There were 204 cities and villages in the three districts of Upper and Lower Galilee and the Valley of Tiberias. It was very rich farming country, and produced olive oil, crafts, fish and fruits which sustained the region and provided valuable exports. Sowing seeds, buying land, hiring workers, observing harvests, seeing the seasons come and go, all formed natural and familiar material for Jesus's teaching.

This self-sufficiency produced a strong spirit of independence. Foreigners were there to be used, but were not welcome. And in Galilee, hopes of establishing a separate state were easy to arouse. From the execution of Ezekias in 47 BC to the execution of Jacob and Simon, sons of Judas, in 48 AD, a steady succession of revolts took place in Galilee, often led by members of the same family of Judas the Galilean. The title 'Galilean' easily became associated with these Zealots. Flavius Josephus, whose book *Jewish Wars* tells us many of these things, was rebel commander-in-chief in the northern region in the Jewish-Roman War of AD 66–70.

Galileans had strong north-country accents, which immediately betrayed them. Peter was recognised, presumably because of his accent (14.70). 'Are not all these Galileans?' the crowd ask in Acts 2.7, indicating their amazement that such unsophisticated provincials could speak in other languages.

Orthodox Judaism was run by southerners. While Jesus had his supporters from Judea and Jerusalem (3.7–8), it is 'scribes, who came down from Jerusalem' who cause Jesus trouble in 3.22 and 7.1.

For Jesus, 'going up to Jerusalem' (10.32,33) meant taking his good news to the hostile authorities. There are ominous tones in Jesus 'drawing near' (11.1), 'entering' (11.11) and 'coming to' (11.15,27) Jerusalem. It is 'the city of the great King' (Mt.5.35), but equally it is the power base of Jesus's enemies.

There is a strong provincialism about Jesus.

His Galilean background, you might say, served him well.

It meant he was a bit free from legalistic religion. It meant he grew up alongside all kinds of people. It meant he knew the way ordinary people thought of the rich, especially those in the capital. It meant he could see victimisation, poverty and discrimination at first hand. It meant he knew the piety of practical people, from the bottom.

Yet, it also restricted him. He could only 'belong' to

one place, and that place was an off-centre region, a cultural backwater, a place neither wholly Israelite nor wholly pagan. Its hopes and expectations would prove to be a problem to him.

And he himself almost from the start seems to have no expectations of the dominant society based on the capital, and only contempt and criticism for most of those who belong to the capital. He is a provincial. For bad as well as for good!

2: Lower Middle Class

Lower middle class seems to be the best contemporary description for Jesus's background.

The upper class, the rulers, were the aristocratic priestly families and the royal households of the Herods. All they had to do was to collect their tithes and taxes. Beside them were the 'elders', the nobility, who owned most of the land. These upper class people were a small elite – probably less than one per cent of the population. Significantly, it was the 'chief priests' and the 'elders' who condemned Jesus (14.53).

The vast majority of people worked on the land. Probably they were ninety per cent of the inhabitants. The per capita income for the one hundred million people in the Roman Empire was around £100 per annum – the figure in the poorest pre-industrial world countries today. It was this vast crowd of people without security that kept the middle class at work, as it would be very easy for them to lose their trade and slip into the labouring poor.

The mass of the common people were regarded as 'sinners' by those above them. 'Sinner' does not mean someone who has intentionally committed a sinful or immoral act. Rather, it means someone who is not within the covenant relationship of the faithful children of Israel. You were a 'sinner' if you had not got pure Jewish ancestry, or if you were illegitimate, or if you had inherited some deformity, sickness or malfunction. If you were a 'sinner', you could not attend the synagogue, learn the Jewish Law, appear as a witness in court, or hold any office or public post. You were 'beyond the pale', an outsider, a marginalised and dependent person without status or place within the society. The word 'sinner' does not describe such people fairly. I shall use phrases like 'people outside the Law' or 'outcasts' (which Today's English Bible uses).

Jesus, obviously, did not belong to the top group or the bottom group, so that in this sense he could be called 'middle class'. Probably, in today's parlance, 'lower middle class' is most accurate. Or, if 'working class' means for you the group of skilled tradespeople or craftsmen who hand on their skills, he was 'upper working class'. Such were Jesus's 'own home place, his own peers and his own family' (6.4). It was this group which contained skilled artisans – blacksmiths, shoemakers, woodcutters, carpenters, tentmakers (like Paul). It was the *'petite bourgeoisie'* group of the day, with a strong interest in keeping the *status quo*, as their living depended on work coming their way from the rich. Yet they had no control on the economy.

Actually, the word used to describe Jesus as a 'carpenter' is better translated 'builder'. The Greek word *tekton* is often used for a 'house builder'. Obviously, as wood was a dominant material in building houses, the builder would also be a carpenter. In small towns, the builder would need a mixture of skills. So he would be someone who could put his hand to many things, an odd-job man, a 'jobbing builder'. He would not be a builder in the modern sense of a manager of others. Rather, he would be a 'one man band', able to put his hand to any building or maintenance job.

If we thus place Jesus in the lower middle class, that does not mean that he belonged to a wealthy family. The offering made for him of 'a pair of turtle doves, or two young pigeons' (Lk.2.22–4) was the offering only made by poor people. As Jesus says, 'People who

17

dress richly are in Kings' houses' (Mt.11.8). Yet they were religious people. They supported the synagogues, and sent their children to learn the Law. Out of their number, people became scribes, pharisees, rabbis, essenes and zealots – the religious denominations of first century Judaism. Apart from the priests and the Sanhedrin, Judaism's religion was firmly rooted in the upper and lower middle class.

Jesus as a lower middle class person clearly got from somewhere his education and his insights into the traditions of his people. This caused people to be astonished at his teaching (1.27) and to reflect on its possible source (6.2–4). Jesus, then, had gained or taught himself sufficient knowledge to be regarded as a legitimate teacher in the congregations (1.21). His status was such as to command the attention of religious authorities from Jerusalem (3.22).

Jesus, the lower middle class lad, had been 'educating himself up', had been spending time in the synagogue and with the Law books. People 'wondered at the gracious words that he spoke' (Lk.4.22). Jesus was a lower middle class lad making his way upwards within the social culture. Soon, he might have been a teacher or a scribe. He might even have become a pharisee or joined the Essenes or become a rabbi. He was on the 'journey upward' which opens up to any lower middle class lad who becomes educated.

According to Luke 3.23, Jesus was around thirty years old when he first appeared in public. Two or three years later, he was crucified. So that leaves the vast majority of his life unknown to us. We usually assume that he worked with Joseph his father as a carpenter for nearly twenty years of his life. But he also clearly used his spare time to learn the Law and become acquainted with the various contemporary opinions about the Law. And he encountered the various political and religious options of his time. All this is clear from the Gospels. But how it all happened belongs to those 'hidden years'.

3: Man of Roots

I shall normally use the word 'radical' in its usual
sense – to mean something or someone extreme, or
thoroughgoing, essential, basic, unconventional, or
total. And Jesus was 'radical' in that sense.

But the word 'radical' comes from a Latin word *radix*
meaning root, or origin. So that radical also has to do
with what is at the root or the base of things. A word
in the English language can be a 'radical' word when
it is itself a root, not derived from any other word. Jesus
was a radical in this sense, too. What he represents is
a 'return', a journey backwards, back and down into
the fundamental story of humanity, as he learned it in
his own heritage and tradition, supremely in the Old
Testament which enshrined the holy Law of his people.
In fact, Jesus has a very radical way of dealing with
the roots of his own nation and its significance.

The first 13 verses of chapter 1 of Mark indicate how
Jesus's story goes back into the roots of Israel's story.

1. The Root of 'Levelling'

'Levelling' means making things level. It is a very
biblical idea, and Mark's Gospel begins with a reference
to a prophecy in Isaiah which the writer sees fulfilled
in John the Baptist.

> A voice crying in the wilderness,
> Make straight a highway for our God
> Every valley shall be brought up

Every mountain and hill brought down
Rugged places shall be made smooth,
Mountain ranges become a plain. (Isaiah 40.3–4)

Mark actually only gives us the beginning of the quotation (1.3), but everyone would know what it means. It is a vast *levelling* operation. Excesses are reduced, inadequacies are made good. John the Baptist conducted a 'levelling' mission – *everybody* came out from all the regions for his baptism (1.4–5). And he lived on a very simple basic level (1.6). Even Jesus is 'levelled' in the water alongside all the rest (1.9). And everyone is told to do the same as everyone else – to 'level things out' (see Lk.3.10–14).

So one of the roots of God's radicalism is hinted at: all God's people are meant to be on the same level, as is his creation. It is a theme that will occur again in Mark's story of Jesus.

2. The Root of Sonship

After his baptism, Jesus receives a heavenly voice: 'You are my son, my beloved. My favour rests on you' (1.11).

To us, this means something like 'Jesus was the Son of God'. But the root idea of Judaism is that all faithful Israelites were the sons and daughters of God. And the reference here is back to the fundamental origin of the people of Israel. They were all slaves in bondage in Egypt, hundreds of years before, and then the miracle of the divine call came. 'Out of Egypt, I called my son' (Hosea 11.1).

The root of Israel and of Jesus is in an experience of being called, being overcome, being compelled, being given a name that was not one's name before. So we get the hint: the roots of God's radicalism lie in the sense of uniqueness, specialness, obligation and filial obedience.

3. The Root of Wilderness

Immediately after his baptism, the Spirit drives Jesus 'away into the wilderness for forty days, tempted by Satan' (1.12). It is the root of Israel, too, forty years wandering in the wilderness, before coming to Palestine, the promised land. Those forty years were the great testing time for the children of Israel. They had to complete their 'Exodus' before they reached their goal (Exodus 16–40). The forty days of Jesus are the testing of Jesus.

The forty days of Jesus seem also to be like a kind of 'return to nature'. 'He is among the wild beasts, and angels wait on him' (1.13). Matthew and Luke describe three temptations, relevant to Jesus's hopes for his mission (Mt.4.1–11, Lk.4.1–13). But Mark only gives us this stark, lonely picture.

There is a root called wilderness, that lies at the base of all history and self-consciousness. Wilderness has to be radically taken into oneself again and again, before there is any promised land or any good news to tell.

In such a grounding in history does Mark place Jesus. It is as if once Jesus starts, the whole of history is to be done all over again. It is as if the basic core of Israel's existence, of God's equal love to all, of God's family and children, of God's wilderness in everyone's soul, is being lived again in the person of Jesus.

And perhaps it is that I, today, am having my life lived again in it, in these roots?

4: Inner City Man

I can't help feeling that Jesus, as we have discovered him so far, would be very at home in my part of the world, in the inner city, in our divided Britain.

Galilee was a land run by aliens. Most of the great landowners did not live in the villages. They came in from outside. They hired others to do their dirty work. Like the man who owned the vineyard in the Parable of 12.1–9, they were absentee landlords.

So, we in the inner city are owned by outsiders. There's no money here. No investment. Actually, there's no work either. The industrialists took their money and ran, some of them long ago, some of them in the 1970's and 1980's.

Galilee was the place where the rich passed through. Over the hill, the great trade route carried spices and oils and gold from the East. They had their own supporting facilities at Tiberias. But Galilee itself was only the backdrop for their labours.

So, we in the inner city, can walk down the hill and look into the brightly coloured stores, with goods from all over the world. But we do not buy many of them. They are bought by the people in the suburbs, whose automobile trade route races through our community.

Galilee had large estates, factories of the earth, which grew abundant produce – figs, olives, grapes, corn. But the locals were kept in poverty. They hung around the market place, on the off chance that they could get a day's work – as in the parable of Mt.20.1–7.

So, we in the inner city wait for the crumbs to fall

from the rich people's tables. There is little work that we ourselves can do. The planners have flattened the old workshops, levelled the old gardens, and put useless surrounds of green grass to confirm our idleness.

Galilee was an enemy occupied country, with an active local resistance movement. It needed resolute and firm government. It was not safe to have many of the occupying army actually living there. But when there was trouble, they came in and took firm reprisals. So, in AD 67, the Roman soldiers marched in to punish the people of Jaffa, and reduced it to rubble, as they had done to Sepphoris when Judas ben Hezekiah set up his revolt in AD 4.

So, the inner city today is a 'no-go' area for police at times. Some of us riot out of frustration, alienation and cynicism. And they come in with their armoured cars, riot shields, helmets and truncheons. They would bring in the army if necessary.

Galilee was a 'marked' country. It was the north, and its north-country people had strong north-country accents. The language they spoke was a crude 'pigeon-Aramaic', scarcely comprehensible to southerners from Jerusalem and Judea.

So, inner city people and people from the north are 'marked' people. Sometimes we have different colour skins. Usually, we have different accents. You can always tell.

Galilee was a powerless province, that produced a firm independence. The religious authorities coming up from Jerusalem might have the power. But the locals had their own religion, and hailed their own prophets. A strongly insular, isolated consciousness resulted. People had to snatch at anything they could, and visitors were 'ripped off' for whatever they might bring. They became emotionally hard. Things will not change – so grab whatever you can.

So, inner city people become hard. We take whatever

we can from whoever comes. We've been taught to wait. And we get into trouble because we do not always say thank you.

Jesus gave Galileans a voice. He heard their cry and made it his own. He took their stories and told them to others. He studied their folk lore, their gossip, their scandals, their loves and their hates – and turned them into parables of the action of God himself! He took their children and said 'Receive kids like these, and you have the Kingdom'. He took their halt and blind and lame and healed them and said 'If you only help these, you help me'.

Jesus gives the inner city a voice now. Nobody else does. But we have got attitudes like the ones he knew, stories like the ones he told, people like the ones he loved and laughed at.

I can only hope Jesus feels as much at home with us as we do with him. That remains to be seen!

To you, with Great Hesitation

Lord Jesus,

Not surprisingly, I begin with many doubts.

You do not seem to inspire confidence. Your northern accent, your workman's hands, your bourgeois background, don't impress me. Your presumption to 'be' Israel is odd, even laughable. Your claims about the Kingdom are far beyond your power to fulfil. I am surrounded with enough odd-balls without you as well!

Actually, you were a disappointment to everybody, weren't you? Your mother had such high hopes for you. Your disciples gave up everything to follow you. Many people thought you'd bring in the Kingdom.

And you disappointed them all.

You bighead! It had to be your own way, or nothing; your own ideas, or none.

You would only be accepted on your own terms.

You were always different. You knew what was expected, and you always did the opposite.

Your critics inspire my sympathy. You could see no good in them at all. But no-one can always be wrong.

You all-or-nothing Jesus. You lose so many by your angularity, your crassness, your insensitivity to fine distinctions, your ignorance of the nuances of sophisticated ways.

If you are right, then everyone else has to be wrong.

If you are right, we shall always be wrong. And only at the odd, fraught, fought-for edges of our existence shall we name you Lord.

Presumably, you know it. Perhaps you rejoice at it.

Lord, let me take you in, indigestible, my enemy, my disappointment. You are at least different enough for me occasionally to think you might at times possibly even be right.

Part Two: Radical Kingdom

It happened that he was sitting at table in his house. Many tax collectors and outcasts from the Law sat down with Jesus and his disciples. There were many of them who were among his followers.

Some teachers of the Law, scribes, who belonged to the party of the Pharisees, saw him eating with these people outside the Law, and tax collectors.

'Why does he eat with tax collectors and "sinners"?', they said to his disciples.

Jesus heard their question and himself replied:

> 'Whole people don't need Doctors.
> It's sick people who need Doctors.
> I didn't come to call those inside the Law,
>   but those outside it.'

Mark 2.15–17

5: Radical Happenings

'What is this?'

'What is this crazy teaching?'

'He's giving orders even to evil spirits, and they obey him.'

The news spreads everywhere about the young man who has suddenly appeared in Nazareth. All over Galilee, they are talking about it.

At night, the people take all their sick people to him, and he heals them and casts out their evil spirits.

Everyone is looking for him, but he almost runs away, 'We've got to give other people a chance as well', he says.

Wherever he goes, the message is the same.

'Everything is happening – this is the hour!' he cries. 'God's Revolutionary Rule is at the door. Change yourselves completely, and trust yourselves to the good news.'

Soon, the implications of what he is saying become clear.

For everyone, it means a complete change of everything.

Different groups of people respond in distinct ways.

For sick people, it means an immediate challenge to the forces and powers which are thought to be responsible for their sickness. In the synagogue, a man has an evil spirit, which screams out, 'What do you want with us, Jesus of Nazareth? Are you here to destroy us? I know who you are – the Holy One of God'. Lying in bed sick with a fever, a mother is raised up. Dozens of sick and demon-possessed people are brought out to him, and he heals many of them and drives out their demons.

To the sick, Jesus is a radical because he breaks through all the old conventions and taboos, and treats them as real people in need. He is the Radical Lover.

For converts, for people wanting to join him, for the few people whom Jesus chooses, the challenge means leaving everything and becoming a disciple. Simon and Andrew are told, 'Come with me and I will teach you to fish for people,' and they leave their nets and go off with him. James and John are called, and they leave their father and their workers, and go off with Jesus. Levi the tax collector is invited, 'follow me', and gets up and follows him.

To the disciples, Jesus is a radical, because he breaks through all their existing loyalties, and demands a total allegiance to himself. He is the Radical Master.

For the people, the ordinary people of the towns and country, Jesus makes no such demands. But they have plenty to concern themselves with about Jesus. From the beginning they are astonished at what he is doing and teaching. 'What is this?', they ask each other. 'What is this new teaching?' 'He even commands demons, and they obey him'. Everywhere in Galilee, the news spreads. Sometimes, everyone in the town turns out to see him. When he tries to get away, his disciples find him and tell him, 'Everyone is looking for you'. Soon, he is talked about everywhere, and he cannot go into the towns at all, so has to stay out in lonely places. But even there people come to him from everywhere. Whatever Jesus does, everyone is completely amazed, and praises God and says 'We have never seen anything like this before'.

To the people, Jesus is a radical because he breaks through all their expectations and confronts them with a leader who is bringing in a revolution in everything. He is the Radical Prophet and Spirit-man.

For outcasts, for the people on the edges of the society, Jesus provides an astonishing opportunity. For the first time in their lives, here is someone who, apparently good and holy in himself, is prepared to move towards them and help them. Lepers are outcasts – they are brought in. Tax collectors are outcasts – they are brought in. Breakers of the Old Testament laws are outcasts – they are brought in. Even people outside the Holy Nation of Israel are brought in. He seems to go out of his way to find 'lost sheep'. And he knows what he is doing, and why. 'Healthy people don't need a doctor. But sick people do. I am not here to call the respectable people, but the outcasts.'

To outcasts, Jesus is a radical because he breaks through all the rules and regulations of the holy people of God, and makes celebrations of wholeness with them. He is the Radical Revolutionary.

For officials, for the religious people, Jesus is a problem. One time, Jesus lets a paralysed man be lowered down on a stretcher, right in the middle of the room where he is teaching. Jesus is so impressed with the faith of the four people who do it, that he says to the man, 'My son, your sins are forgiven'. Some teachers of the Law are there, and they reflect, 'Only God can forgive sins. How dare he pretend to be God!' But Jesus says to them that forgiving sins and telling the man to get up and walk are much the same thing. On another occasion, Jesus goes back home with Levi the tax collector. Many tax collectors and other law-breakers follow Jesus, and share a meal with him and his disciples. Some teachers of the law, Pharisees, see this, and put his disciples on the spot about it.

To officials of the religious and social system, Jesus is a radical because he breaks down all the long established and carefully constructed laws. He is the Radical Lawbreaker.

All these incidents I have quoted so far come in Mark 1.14–2.17. It is an amazing procession of different kinds of people, all provoking responses from Jesus, each one related to their own needs and situations.

Each group has its own interest in Jesus, and each group has its own part in the story of Jesus. To each group, Jesus has much to say. In later chapters, we will look at them more. In fact, from Mark 2.18, all the different groups feature one after the other, and often are in conflict within the same story. Jesus's work, teaching and destiny emerge in his everyday activity with them.

6: Radical Manifesto

Jesus never wrote a book. And Jesus never wrote a manifesto. All the pieces of the things he said were memorised and handed on from mouth to mouth. This does not mean that they were not often accurately remembered. People in his culture learned scripture by heart. Possibly Jesus taught his disciples to learn by heart. Even if he didn't, they were present with him often enough and heard him use the same expressions in dealing with different people and situations.

Also, the Gospel we are following in this book, by Mark, does not contain any systematic teaching. According to Matthew 5–7, Jesus preached a longish 'Sermon on the Mount'. According to Luke 6.17–49, some of the same words were used in a 'Sermon on the Plain'. But Mark has hardly any of these sayings.

Yet it is Mark who, in most scholars' view, is plainest about the mission of Jesus and its demands on others.

And it is from Mark that we get the clearest and simplest statements about the message.

The manifesto itself is declared right at the beginning, in 1.14.

> The times are fulfilled
> The Kingdom of God is at the door
> Change yourselves completely
> And trust yourselves to the good news

There it is – Jesus's manifesto.
It's worth taking it bit by bit.

33

1. *'The times are fulfilled.'* For centuries, the people of Israel have been waiting. Surely, God will in the end do something different and decisive. The Old Testament has encouraged people to wait and hope. Now, Jesus claims, the times of waiting and hoping are completed, are at an end. Now, claims Jesus, it's all going to happen.

2. *'The Kingdom of God is at the door.'* In the Old Testament, God is the King of Israel. 'The Lord reigns,' proclaim some of the Psalms, like 93, 97, and 99. But it doesn't *look* as if God is the King. The Romans are in charge, the country is despoiled by foreigners, the Holy Law is ignored, the prophets and holy ones are killed. How can God be King? The Kingdom of God is at the door, says Jesus – Wait and see what it is!

3. *'Change yourselves completely.'* Your ideas, your ways of life, your commitments, your world-views, your attitudes – all of them are now wrong, or at least inappropriate. You need to change completely, if you are going to get a glimpse of this Kingdom. Our word 'repent' has come to mean something more restricted, but 'change yourselves completely' is what the Greek word (*metanoia*) means.

4. *'Trust yourselves to the good news.'* Our word 'believe' does not quite get the force of the Greek word here. It really means 'Give yourself over to', 'risk your life on', 'put your faith in', 'trust yourself to'. So, Jesus says, don't hold yourself back. You will not get anything that way. Rather, let yourself go, 'get with it', take a chance, act as if it was true. The 'good news' is that the Kingdom is here. Let yourselves start acting as if it is true.

This simple but devastatingly total 'manifesto' is

what Jesus preached, and what he taught his disciples to preach.

If this is Jesus's message, it's not much like the so-called 'gospel' of the revivalist preachers, is it? Actually, Jesus is not like them at all. He does not preach that people should change inwardly, first, as if everything would then be alright. By continually stressing inward change, inward conversion, change of heart, change of motives, we have denuded the Gospel. They think that because they have decided to change that the change has actually taken place. They actually continue to do exactly what they did before, but claim that they are 'really' different inwardly, even though no outward evidence is present!

Jesus suggests that people change only when they have to. And people only change when there are situations in which they *have* to be different. Jesus implies that people who wish to change must find areas, commitments, groups, actions, which require and expect them to behave differently. Discipleship to Jesus provides 'strait jackets' whereby people could not do anything else but behave differently. His followers get to change 'inwardly', because they have to become accustomed to doing things in different areas and ways, which demand that they behave differently. My experience today is that churches only change when they have their backs to the wall – that is, when they have to!

So they become 'converted' by being into things which they could only stay in if they were in fact 'converted'! Inwardly, they are still people who want to be cosseted, comforted, supported, praised, and built up in their selfishness. Jesus said 'Do as you would be done by' (Mt.7.12). That is, face it that you are basically selfish and avaricious, and you basically like to be treated well. So treat others as if they are the same. Jesus thus wants us to be as covetous for another

35

person's right to be well done by, as we are thirsty with
our own desire to be well done by.

7: Liberation from Bondage

'Those who are well don't need a doctor. Only sick people need a doctor.' So says Jesus in 2.17. So Jesus happily suggests the idea that he is like a doctor.

Healing is the first 'sign' of the Kingdom. Having gone into the synagogue at Capernaum to teach, a man with an unclean spirit cries out, and Jesus silences it (1. 21–28). Getting to Simon's house for lunch, he finds his mother-in-law sick, so he raises her up (1.29–31). At evening, people bring out all the sick and demon-possessed, and he heals and exorcises many (1.32–34). The next morning, everyone is looking for him, probably because of his healing, but he decides to go elsewhere (1.35–39). Before he is able to do so, a leper begs to be made clean, and Jesus obliges (1.40–45).

The picture is clear. Healing is only one part of Jesus's work. 'I must go and preach elsewhere.' That is what he wants to do (1.38). But people keep putting the sick in front of him, and he can't help being 'moved with compassion', so he heals them (1.41). In the midst of teaching, people even lift a roof off and lower a palsied man down in front of him (2.1–12). He goes into the synagogue to teach, and there is a man with a withered hand (3.1–6). He even gets into a boat, to speak to the people, and to get away from people with plagues 'pressing on him that they might touch him' (3.7–12). He finally gets to deliver some teaching – about parables – only by sitting in a boat (4.1). But the healings continue, one of them even by a woman securing healing without Jesus's intention (5.25–34).

Mark thus records Jesus as a healer who does not come in from outside as the big strong magician, looking for sick people on whom he can demonstrate his divine power. Rather, he appears as someone who at times runs away from his healing powers, and who has to be laid hold of by the sick or their friends, in order to ensure that he heals them. 'If you wanted to, you could heal me' is the cry of the leper in 1.40.

'Your faith has healed you', he says (5.34, 10.52, cf.5.36). Not Jesus, not God, not some special power, but 'faith' causes healing. 'For anyone who has faith, everything is possible', he says (9.23). Whatever you say, as long as you have faith that it will happen, it will' (11.23) – indeed, it already has happened (11.24). If, like Peter, you lose faith, you are lost (14.27–31). Hold on to whatever faith you have, he says to Jairus (5.36). Help my non-faith, the father of the epileptic boy says (9.24). For where there is non-faith, nothing can happen (6.5–6).

Thus, there seems to have been a healing potential in Jesus which lies dormant unless the faith potential in people calls it forth. The Kingdom of God means that this potential of faith is now present in people, and this potential for healing is now present in Jesus, the agent for the Kingdom.

In this sense, Jesus is the liberator.

But he is a totally alternative kind of liberator. He is surrounded by people living in hideous bondage to all kinds of sickness, disease, incapacity and disadvantage. Surely a place for the liberator to go in as the Knight in Shining Armour! Surely a place for the liberator to go in and slaughter all the enemies!

But Jesus does not do it.

From far away, deep inside the poor, the sick and the lame and the blind, there has to swell up a seed.

From out of the gutter, has to come the pearl of great price. Out of nowhere has to come the precious impossibility called 'faith'. And faith is the gleam of hope, trust, life, expectation, determination, anger, bitterness, self-love, or whatever – whatever will move you to demanding a radical change for yourself.

So, people have the power, the potential, within themselves to be made whole, now that the kingom is here, and Jesus, its agent, is before you.

What is 'faith'?

I suggest the reader reads some of the stories, to discover what actually happens in the people, the 'reaching out' that allows Jesus to heal. In 1.40–45, it is the leper's insistence that if Jesus wishes, he could make him clean. In 2.1–12, it is the insight, boldness, imagination, practical activity, whatever it is that becomes visible in taking the roof off and lowering the friend down (see verse 5: It is *their* faith Jesus sees). In 3.1–6, it is the man coming out to the front, and holding out his hand. In 4.40, it is the disciples' lack of faith that is criticised after their panic in the storm at sea. In 5.25–34, a woman with a bleeding grabs hold of his coat, and is healed. In 5.36, it is Jairus's conviction that Jesus can heal his daughter that he has to hold on to. In 10.52, Jesus says simply 'It is your faith that has made you well' to blind Bartimaeus at Jericho. At 11.22, he says 'have faith in God' to Peter, as if that would help them to wither fig trees. It is the 'lack of faith' of 'this generation' in 9.19 which prevents the epileptic boy being healed.

8: Power to the People

People in Jesus's day lived in a world of spirits, demons and supernatural powers. Some of the most powerful stories are stories of demon possession and demon exorcism. It is a part of the story of Jesus which is strange to us today. But there are many parts of the world where demons and demon-possession are present-day realities. And on the fringes of our so-called secular western world, there are instances of demon-possession, 'Satanism', black magic, and spiritism.

According to Mark, 'They brought out all who were ill or demon-possessed' (1.32), 'and he went all through Galilee, casting out devils' (1.39). There are four exorcism stories. 1. A man in the synagogue has an evil spirit in him who cries out 'What do you want with us, Jesus of Nazareth? Are you here to destroy us? I know who you are – God's holy one' (1.24). Jesus speaks to the demon, and casts him out, and people observe his authority over demons (1.27). 2. The madman in 5.1–17, similarly, has devils within him who beg Jesus not to punish them (5.7), but are driven out into pigs, they calling themselves 'legion', but then end up drowning. 3. A Phoenician woman has a daughter who has a demon, which she gets Jesus to cast out by her cleverness (7.24–30). 4. A boy has an evil spirit which throws him into a fit as soon as he sees Jesus, but is then cast out (9.14–29).

Similarly, Jesus sends out his disciples with 'authority over demons' (6.7), and they 'drive out many demons, and pour oil on many and heal them' (6.13).

Perhaps the most dramatic story is that in 3.20–30. His family set out to get Jesus back, as people are saying 'He has gone crazy'. Being crazy means being demon-possessed, and some are saying:

'He has Beelzebul in him,'
'It is the head devil who gives him power to drive other devils out'.

Jesus pours ridicule on this by pointing out that if a country or a family is fighting against itself, it will totally collapse.

What in fact has happened, says Jesus, is that somebody bigger than either the Head Devil or the other devils has arrived. And he has tied up the Head Devil, and thus can plunder his house (3.27).

Moreover, Jesus goes on, it is totally impossible to do anything about someone who, faced with an activity of God, sees Satan in it (3.28–30).

Thus, Jesus describes himself as the one who has overcome the powers of evil in the world. The demons are terrified and crying out because they know their end has come.

Jesus brings power 'out of his own being' – that is what the word *ex-ousia* in 1.27 means. Thus he gives 'power to the people' as they are then able to function in their own power, rather than being subject to alien powers. They also then have power 'in their own being.'

9: Solidarity with the Poor

Jesus, as we saw in the last chapter, could have made a good scribe or pharisee. He is a lower-middle class man, getting education, and on his journey upwards. Yet he makes an 'option for the poor', and even becomes labelled as 'the mate of tax-collectors and outcasts' (Lk.7.34). This is the man who turns his back on his own family and its status and connections, and declares a new family consisting of 'whoever does the will of God' (3.34–35). And he is only able to do so by being prepared to be regarded by them as crazy (3.21), and refusing their claims on him (3.31–33).

Yet, from the very beginning of his ministry, Jesus makes the members of the third class, the under-class, the concern of his work. He calls fishermen, marginal people who are not renowned for keeping the law (1.16–20), plus a tax-collector, specifically excluded from the community of Israel (2.13–14). He heals demon-possessed people (1.23, 1.32), a leper (1.40), a paralytic (2.3). He sits down to a meal with the tax collector Levi and other tax collectors and others outside the Law (2.15). In reply to criticism he declares his programme:

It is not the healthy that need a doctor, but the sick.
I have not come to call the keepers of the Law,
But those whom the Law excludes (2.17).

The implication is clear. Jesus, himself belonging to the lower middle craftsman class, calls as disciples those who are of similar origins, though perceptibly lower on the social scale. But he makes the object of his ministry those who by profession, condition or inheritance are outside the law-abiding middle group. This social 'journey downwards' Jesus understands as his mission, his project.

Jesus, then, finding himself the champion of the ninety per cent, the common people, makes another journey downwards. The common people who hear him gladly (12.37) are not needy enough. Instead of becoming the champion of the common person, the labourers, the victimised within the system, he takes a further step. He turns away from them (6.30–46), calling them 'an evil generation' (Lk. 11.29).

He seeks out the hungry, the halt, the lame and the blind. His 'little flock' is to be the deprived, the especially excluded (Lk. 12.32). He finds his true Kingdom co-partners in those who, like him, have nowhere to lay their heads (Lk.9.58). The Pharisees call them 'the rabble who know nothing of the law' (Jn.7.49).

And they, the riff-raff, the offscouring, the tax collectors and the prostitutes will go into the Kingdom before the chief priests and elders (Mt.21.31). Jesus himself takes the lowest place with them (Lk.14.8–11), to feast with them (Lk.14.13).

A new commonwealth is established through this fellowship with people at the bottom. If you complain that they are socially your enemies, then you are told: 'love your enemies' (Lk.6.35). The test of socially responsible behaviour is now purely and simply: how did you treat the people at the bottom? (Cf. Mt. 25.31–46.)

The solidarity with the poor creates indeed a new alliance of all kinds of people. The Gospels use various names for them:

1. *Beggars*
   Lepers
   Deaf and dumb
   Blind
   Crippled
   Lame
   Possessed

2. *'Sinners'*
   Mixed race
   Illegitimates
   Prostitutes
   Tax-men
   Usurers
   Herdsmen
   Illiterates
   Uneducated

3. *Dependent*
   Widows
   Orphans
   Day labourers
   Slaves

4. *Deprived*
   The persecuted
   The downtrodden
   The captives
   The labouring and heavy
   laden
   The hungry
   The weeping
   Lost sheep
   The little ones
   The least
   The last

Once one is anywhere within these four categories, it is hard to get out. You are 'unclean', that is, unable to fulfil the Law. To become clean, you would have to go through an elaborate process of repentance and cleansing, and then make atonement by paying money. But you cannot use ill-gotten money so you are trapped. And you cannot then be accepted in the synagogue, as you are not educated in the Law.

What Jesus is saying is: The scribes and Pharisees have *made* the people into sinners. But they are not sinners. They are *sinned-against*. The guardians of the Law sin by sinning against the people who are weaker than themselves, by 'binding heavy burdens, grievous to bear' (Mt.23.4). The poor are the sinned-against and

Jesus sides with them, so that he, too, by his solidarity with them, is himself the sinned-against, and excluded from Israel.

10: Parties in Houses

Feasting is important in life.

In religions, shared meals are vital occasions. The Jewish people always regard eating together as the centre of family and community life. Most of the essential rituals are done around the dining table or the kitchen table. Therefore, elaborate rules are developed to ensure that the meals are properly cooked, that only the proper meat is used, and that nothing and nobody 'impure' is allowed to spoil the mealtime.

So that the people with whom a person shares meals is a good indicator of the character of that person. We judge someone by the company they keep. And the contemporaries of Jesus make sure that if they are trying to keep up the Laws of Moses, then they will not allow people who will defile the mealtime to be present.

It is not surprising therefore that Jesus chooses mealtimes as a time to demonstrate his radicality.

Feasting constitutes a major element in the story of Jesus. He feasts with Levi and his friends (2.15–17). His disciples do not fast, but live as the guests at a wedding – that is, they feast (2.18–20). There is new wine, needing new wineskins (2.22). Even in the fields, they help themselves to corn (2.23–26). Another time, the crowd collects 'so that they have no chance to eat' – as if eating is important (3.20). Jairus's daughter, raised up, gets 'something to eat' (5.43). 'No leisure even to eat' comes again at 6.31. Eating is a major question in the feeding of the 5,000 (6.30–44) and the

4,000 (8.1–10), with their great open-air banquets, and basketfuls of surplus. The odd discussion about the disciples taking bread with them (8.14–21) is a key passage: Jesus himself provides the bread. 'Take the bread: it is my body' (14.22) is the final stage.

It is possible that it is Jesus's own house in which the feasts took place. Or it could have been a house shared with Simon and Andrew and Simon's mother-in-law (1.29–31). 'He was at home' (2.1) is often taken as meaning Jesus's home. 'His house' at 2.15 could mean Levi's house or Jesus's. If it were Jesus's, then Jesus as the prophet entertaining 'bad characters, tax collectors and others', would be even more striking.

'The Son of Man comes eating and drinking, and you say, look, a glutton and a drunkard, a mate of tax-collectors and sinners', is Jesus's comment in Lk.7.34. 'I piped, but you wouldn't dance' (Lk.7.32) is Jesus's complaint.

All this must have been intentional on Jesus's part. As Jesus was often called a 'prophet', people would know that you have to watch what a prophet does as much as listen to what a prophet says. A prophet performs 'prophetic signs' or 'acted parables'. They are dramatic and striking ways by which the prophets in the Old Testament – and Jesus, clearly – put into actions what they conceived God's mission and God's demand to be.

And the location of Jesus's happenings, the happenings of the Kingdom, must be significant. Jesus's first healings and teachings are done in the synagogue. But after chapter 6 the house replaces the synagogue. At 5.21–24, 35–43, the synagogue ruler significantly gets a healing in his house. Thereafter, the house and the disciples replace the synagogue and the scribes as locations and questioners (7.17; 9.28,33; 10.10). And the house becomes the location of ministry by Jesus (7.24) and to Jesus (14.3–9). The Temple is now about to be destroyed (13.2) and the synagogue rejected (13.9). There is now a new place for the holy activities of Temple and synagogue – the house.

And the new activity for the new place is meals and talk, feasting and learning – parties! The Kingdom is for everyone, but until they know it, then those who do know it must enjoy it on their own – or bring in others, whether they understand or not, as Jesus in Luke 14.12–14 demands.

So, until the great Party in the Kingdom some day soon, Jesus and his Community now in his lifetime, and now in the 1980's, celebrate as they can. The Party at your house on Sunday hopefully is a foretaste of eating in the Kingdom (Lk.14.15), of the marriage feast of the Lamb (Rev.19.9).

11: Partnership with Women

Jesus lives in what we today would call a very sexist society. Male and female roles are very clearly delineated. No crossing of the barriers between acceptable male and female behaviour is encouraged.

In this area also, Jesus proves to be a radical. Reluctantly, living in a sexist society, he has to adhere to many of its customs. Accordingly, the degree to which the Jesus story stakes out new ground in partnership with women is truly astonishing. It is a real source of encouragement today to people of both sexes trying to set right the long inequalities of history.

Jesus's partnership with women is visible in Mark's Gospel in five ways:

1. Jesus deals with women in need. In Simon's house, Jesus finds his mother-in-law sick and raises her up so that she is well and able to minister to them (1.29–31). Outcasts, people excluded by the Law (2.16–17) would certainly often include women. The daughter of Jairus is healed (5.21–4; 35–43). And a woman with a haemorrhage for twelve long years grabs Jesus's cloak and her bleeding stops (5.25–34). At 6.56, people take their sick so they might at least touch the hem of his garment. Presumably the general reference to sick people always includes women.

2. Individual actions by women are hailed by Jesus. In Tyre, a foreign port, Jesus is escaping publicity and is apprehended by a Syro-Phoenician woman whose

49

daughter has a demon. Jesus exorcises the demon in response to the woman's smart reply when he ungenerously describes non-Jews as 'dogs' (7.24–30). The widow's offering (12.41–44) is singled out by Jesus in the Temple as she has put in 'all that she had, all she had to live on' (v.44). In the home of Simon the leper, a woman with a jar of expensive perfume pours it over Jesus's head (14.3–9). Jesus says, 'She prepared my body for burial.' Her story is to be told 'wherever the Gospel is preached.'

3. *Women minister alongside Jesus and the disciples.* Some women, including Salome, Mary Magdalene and Mary the mother of the younger James and of Joses are at the cross (15.40), and Mark says:

> They had followed Jesus when he was in Galilee, and ministered with him. Many other women were also there who had come down to Jerusalem with them (15.41).

Mary Magdalene, Mary the mother of James and Salome bring spices to anoint Jesus's body (16.1). Lk.8.1–3 lists a larger group 'who were ministering together with him out of what they had'. A vital women's disciple group is clear.

4. *Jesus has strained relations with his mother.* Jesus's mother appears in Mark for the first time in 3.31–35, when she and his brothers arrive to take him home, as people were saying he was mad (3.21). Jesus replies that 'my brother and sister and mother' are those who fulfil the wishes of God. In 6.3, Jesus's sisters are mentioned. Jesus cares that the relations and family of a prophet do not accept him (6.4). Yet neglect of parents is exposed in 7. 9–13 where Jesus condemns

people who give to God (or the Temple) what could help their father or mother.

5. *Jesus protects the rights of married women*. Divorce was mainly by men against women. The Pharisees' question about divorce (10.7–9) leads Jesus to emphasise God's original intention in making male and female – that the two may become one. Jesus follows this by sharp criticism of 'putting away' a partner to marry another. The trick question of Sadducees (12.18–27) concerning a woman who is married to seven brothers in succession is answered in totally non-sexist terms.

Usually, Luke is thought of as showing Jesus's special concern for women, and it is true that he has some striking stories – the widow of Nain's son (Lk.7.12–15), the woman bent double (Lk.13.10–17), the sinful woman anointing Jesus's feet (Lk.7.36–50), the woman who shouts from the crowd (Lk. 11.27–8), and Mary and Martha (Lk.10.38–42). John alone has the woman caught in adultery (Jn.7.53–8.11), the woman at the well (Jn.4.1–42) and Mary, Martha and Lazarus (Jn.11.1–44).

Jesus's radical claim and action for the equality and partnership of women is clear in all the Gospels. He pioneers new relationships, and the power of his pioneering attitude in this area has still not come to fruition. Strikingly, Mark's Gospel ends with the command to the women to take the news to Galilee. 'There you will see him' (16.7), says the young man, and though it all ends with the women afraid to say anything (16.8), we know that the news did get out, and presumably they let it out.

12: Success to the Struggle

Mark's Gospel shows us a Jesus who spends a great deal of his time running away from a popular movement, perhaps a potential revolt which saw him as its leader.

From the beginning, Jesus is constantly besieged by people bringing their sick to him. Jesus cannot openly enter into any city, but has to stay outside in desert places. Even there, they come to him from all parts of the country (1.45). A little later, Jesus withdraws to the sea, but a great crowd follow from Galilee, Judea, Jerusalem, Idumea, beyond Jordan, and from Tyre and Sidon (3.7–8). The crowd is so big on another occasion that he gets into a boat to speak to them (4.1). At 6.7–13 he sends the twelve disciples out to preach and exorcise (3.14), which they do successfully (6.30). Five thousand chase Jesus into a desert place, where they are taught 'many things' (6.34) and fed with loaves and fish. Five thousand men. They have clearly gathered together to try to secure Jesus as leader for some kind of popular movement or even rebellion. Jesus is able to send them away quickly, and thus inevitably turns away from such a leadership role.

At 7.24–30, Jesus seems to want to run away from Galilee, and the crowds. At 7.24–30, he is in Tyre and Sidon, then in 7.31 in the Decapolis beyond Jordan. Back in Galilee, four thousand spend three days with him and are fed (8.1–10) – presumably in Mark's view another attempt to secure him as leader – possibly Gentiles. At 8.27, Jesus takes his disciples away from

Galilee again, up towards Mount Hermon, to the Roman city of Caesarea Philippi.

At Caesarea Philippi, Peter makes the statement that Jesus is the Christ. The word *Christos* is the Greek translation from the Hebrew 'Messias'. And 'Messias' means 'anointed one'. All the kings of Israel were 'anointed', made special by the oil of anointing. But the 'anointed one' was, people believed, the special one who was going to bring in the Kingdom of God. And what could that mean but that the inaugurator of the Kingdom was himself a King?

Jesus himself clearly does not want to be the leader of the people in the sense in which they desire it. Yet he is their champion, and many of his sayings and actions must bring great satisfaction to the hearts of his own people. When he outwits the Pharisees from Jerusalem, or debates with the authorities, they feel 'Good for him. At last we have someone who does them down at their own game.'

So, Jesus makes his 'triumphal entry'. The Galilean champion has his little band of followers, 'running in front of him and behind him' (11.9). They are not many, and it is the little band of camp-followers from Galilee, not hordes of Jerusalem bystanders, who cry:

> Hosanna!
> Blessings on him
> Who comes in the name of the Lord
> Blessings on the Kingdom that is coming,
>   our father David's Kingdom
> Hosanna in the highest (11.9–10).

The next day, Jesus returns to 'cleanse' the Temple. Soon, the chief priests, scribes and elders demand to know on what authority he is acting (11.27–33). But Jesus 'occupies' the Temple and teaches there (chapter 12). His opponents seek to lay hold on him, 'but they fear the crowd' (12.12). The common people, presumably the people of Jerusalem, 'hear him gladly' (12.37).

The cause of Jesus's condemnation is uncertain. False witnesses appear, Jesus admits to being 'the Messiah, the Son of the Blessed' (14.62), but Pilate 'perceives that the chief priests had delivered him up out of envy' (15.10). Why envy? Presumably because Jesus has the people behind him – as is implied by the elaborate arrangements made for Jesus to be handed over to them, and also the night of haste with which Jesus was judged first by Jewish and then by Roman authorities (14.53–15.15). Almost before his Galilean supporters would be out of bed, Jesus is condemned to crucifixion. At the third hour (9 a.m.) he is crucified (15.25).

What has happened?

Jesus seems to have expected it, and even to have willed it.

Somehow, it seems right, fitting. It seems to have been success for what he wanted.

13: Welcome to Foreigners

Jesus is a Jew, and so are his disciples. But the story in Mark tells us of a gradual but growing openness to people outside Judaism.

Once Jesus reaches the other side of the lake (5.1), he is in Gentile territory, where pigs, the symbol of Gentile uncleanness, are (5.11), and two thousand pagan devils (5.9) are despatched. The healed man preaches in the Ten Gentile Cities (5.20). Later, Jesus takes another trip (6.45–52) to 'the other side', where many healings take place (6.53–56), again in Gentile territory. The food taboos of Jews are exposed, and the welcome to non-taboo Gentiles is clear (7.1–23).

Then Jesus goes away along the Gentile mediterranean coast, hoping for a holiday, away from the crowds. But then in Tyre a Syro-Phoenician woman finds him, challenges his description of Gentiles as dogs, and secures the healing of her daughter (7.24–30). Jesus then continues his tour in Gentile areas, in the Decapolis (7.31), where the deaf mute is healed (7.32–37), after which four thousand are fed (8.1–9). The 'seven' in the story in verses 5, 6, and 8 refers to Gentiles, perhaps recalling the seven Hellenists of Acts 6.1–6.

Mark's Gospel was written, many today think, to Christians in Gentile, non-Jewish churches. Some of the references in chapter 13 seem to refer to the great Revolt of AD 66–70 in Palestine. So somewhere in those years, Mark (whoever he was) wrote down the first and most striking summary of the 'good news' (or

'Gospel'). His 'good news' is the heart and origin of the whole Christian movement.

Mark wrote in a fairly crude way. The Greek he wrote in was called the *Koine*, which comes from the root *koinos*, meaning 'something shared by everyone'. It was the language of tradespeople, travellers, and people living in mixed settlements, at the eastern end of the Mediterranean. Mark indicates that he knows bits of Aramaic and Hebrew, but he also tends to translate them, as if the readers do not know a great deal about Jewish things. So, too, he adds explanatory notes about Jewish customs.

Many think that Mark wrote to the early Christians in Rome. If he did, then we can imagine the situation. All sorts of people from all sorts of backgrounds belonged to the Church there, as we can see from Paul's Epistle to the Romans, 16.1–23. Romans was probably written around AD 45. Afterwards, in AD 64, the Christians had been blamed by the mad emperor Nero for his own setting fire to the city of Rome. Nero made living torches out of some of the Christians. Possibly at this time, AD 64–67, Peter and Paul also perished in Rome.

So that Mark's 'good news' would have come to his readers as an urgent recall to their fundamental commitment. That commitment was to a Lord, whom they called Son of God, who had appeared in Galilee, bringing deliverance to people similar to themselves – frightened, excluded, marginalised, dispossessed. Christians in Rome could easily identify with them, as they did not even belong clearly to Rome or to Judaism. Their Lord was a rival to Caesar as Lord, their Messiah was an affront to Judaism.

Their Lord also seemed to know about things which faced them. That is the purpose of Mark 13. Not a stone of the Temple will be left upon another (13.2). There will be wars, rumours of wars, and famines –

like the Jewish War of 66–70 (13.7–8). People will betray each other (13.9), and torture, trials and executions will follow (13.10–13). Readers are invited to understand what 'the abomination of desolation' is (13.14) – perhaps the profanation of the Temple in AD 70, or some earlier horror. As after the fall of Jerusalem in AD 70 people flee to the mountains, pursued by the Roman legions (13.15–20).

Yet, says Mark, that is not the time for the Messiah to appear (13.21–23). It will be after that distress that sun, moon, stars and heavenly powers will change and the Son of Man will come in the clouds, to gather in his chosen ones (13.24–27). So, the message to the readers is: hold on, don't think that the current tragedies are the end of the world. For the end of the world is only when the Son of Man will come to your rescue.

Mark 13.30 says: 'the present generation will live to see it'. In fact, the end of the world does not happen then. Some people think that Jesus himself thinks the end of the world will come soon after his resurrection. Mark obviously thinks that Jesus is saying that it will happen soon after AD 70.

Neither proves right.

Or at least, neither prove right historically. But if you take some of these words as being 'apocalyptic', then you can get more out of them. Apocalyptic writing is in the Old Testament, the inter-testamental literature, and in the New Testament (like the Book of Revelation). Its purpose is to show, how in the end, Jesus or God would triumph. Hence, if you are going through hell – and apocalyptic was always written when the nation or church was going through hell – then you can cheer up, because your redemption is near. So, you need to be vigilant (13.33), and 'stay awake' (13.37).

So: the foreigners in Rome, in the end, get again the Kingdom that Jesus first gives to his Gentile contemporaries.

Jesus, Why Don't You Go Back Home?

Jesus,

Why don't you go back home?

Haven't you caused enough trouble already?

Don't you see that even if a few people get sat on, it is better that the whole of society keeps going?

It's a test of morality to ask: Can this conduct be universalised? What would happen if everyone did what you do?

And it's no good you saying that you are special, because you call us disciples to do what you do.

For a start, you seem to take it for granted that there will be some good people who keep everything going, so that you and your disciples can play your games on the edges of things.

You couldn't actually make a whole world out of the poor, the outcasts, the tax collectors, the prostitutes, the halt, the lame and the blind. . . .

Are you really content that your whole mission should be tied up with people like that?

Isn't this supposed to be the Kingdom of God? Shouldn't everybody be in it? You seem to be so selective. And what an odd selection!

And what do you think God thinks about it all? Is he content that his majesty and holiness should be poured out like this?

And what do you think people today think about it, trying to keep society together, trying to maintain law and order, trying to maintain some standards from the past?

Now, We Need You Now

Radical Jesus,
You preferred the poor and outcast,
You regarded women and men as equals,
You told people to leave all to follow you,
You rejected established religious ideas,
You opposed authorities and powers,
You were homeless and led a wandering life.
We need you now.

We in Britain in the 1980s
We need you now.

We have the poor and outcast;
    You are among them.
We still have women oppressed;
    You are for them.
We have people giving up what they have;
    You sustain them.
We have people questioning old religious ideas;
    You are on their side.
We have tiny groups resisting authorities and
    powers;
    Your spirit is with them.
We have homeless and wanderers by choice;
    Your way crosses theirs.

Our problem is:–
Not that you are irrelevant to Britain in the 1980s –
But that most of us have too many vested interests
    which are threatened by you;
Not that we do not need your dramatic reversals of
    our ideas and commitments –
But that we would have to change.

And we could change.

So we are calling for change,
   in ourselves,
   in everyone,
   in everything,
As you did.
And we are inviting people to join us
In a company of people committed to finding what
   your way means today.

Part Three: Radical Destiny

Everyone is going to be salted with fire.

> Salt is good.
>> But if salt loses its saltiness,
>> You cannot make it salty again.

> You need the salt in you.
> And be at peace with one another.

Jesus
Mark 9.49–50

14: Alternative

If you consider your own life, your own existence, then you can sometimes amuse yourself by listing the things which are important to you. I did this on an Autumn Saturday recently, clearing up the winter leaves and tidying the garden. I concluded, not very surprisingly, that the things which I most valued in life were:
1. My wife and children
2. The house I live in especially the study
3. Close friends and colleagues
4. My books and my ideas
5. My commitment to causes and pioneering

These are not necessarily in order of importance. But they are the things to which I am fundamentally committed, both as a person and as a disciple of Christ.

When I look at Jesus, it's all so different, and I have to begin to account for the fact that I am a disciple of Jesus at all. On every point he does not represent what is important to me:
1. He has no wife or children, and leaves his mother and relatives.
2. He has no place to lay his head, and only the desert for a study.
3. He has twelve disciples, but they are hardly close friends or colleagues.
4. He has no books, and apparently only read Old Testament scriptures.
5. He has a commitment to the kingdom, which in fact proves incommunicable in terms of a cause he can pioneer for others.

Therefore, in anything I have to do with Jesus, I have to turn everything on its head. If I am to be a disciple of Jesus, I have to face it that my master does not represent the things which I regard as important. He represents a completely different lifestyle and scale of values.

Moreover, when I study his teaching, he seems to go out of his way to repudiate the very things which I regard as precious. Just consider some of his statements which relate to my five most valued areas:

1. He who has left father, mother, wife, children. . . . (10.29)
   He who loves father or mother more than me is not worthy of me. (Mt. 10.37)
2. If anyone would come after me, let them deny themselves, take up their cross and follow me. (8.34)
3. Do not trust those who say 'Lo here,' (13.21)
4. Be not called rabbi or master, for one is your master, even Christ. (Mt. 23.8)
5. Seek first the kingdom of God, and its righteousness, and all the rest will be added to you. (Mt. 6.33)

– But the Kingdom is presumably what Jesus has – and that merely takes us back to his lifestyle.

Jesus emerges out of his time as the classic Alternative. In Mark's Gospel at least, he seems to say 'No' to almost every role, title and place. He refuses to answer most questions. When he explains, it is in riddles. He constantly exposes his disciples, but rarely clarifies anything to them. He blames them for not understanding anything – but he rarely explains himself.

It is as if whatever anybody else around him is into, he is into something different. Whatever anyone else is bothered with, he has a different agenda. Whatever questions come, he is answering something else.

Whatever people are looking for, he is offering something different.

He is the Alternative – the Alternative Messiah (the 'crucified one'), the Alternative Human ('Son of Man'), the Alternative Rabbi and Teacher ('Whence has he received?'), the Alternative 'Lord' (a servant). The Gospel he proclaims is not 'something you can do': it is something you have to allow to happen and then to get in on. The Gospel is not 'something to believe in', it is something to throw yourself upon.

Jesus the Alternative.

15: Guru

Every year, a few hundred people trickle out of Britain, going east, to seek wisdom. There are thirty thousand West German people, mainly in their twenties and thirties, in India. They went to escape from the burdens of the lifestyle of the West. Many of them went to find a guru, a teacher, a master, a wise man (usually male!), at whose feet they might sit, and into whose view of life they might enter.

Eastern religions especially concentrate on the idea of the guru or wise man. Sometimes, the guru is to be found at an Ashram. And there are Christian Ashrams with Christian gurus, more often with small Christian communities as hosts, helpers and interpreters.

No-one would confuse the Urban Theology Unit in Sheffield with an eastern Ashram, or its staff with gurus! Yet, many of the people, young and old, who come to us are looking for the instruction and guidance (which they get) and the discipline and control (which they don't get!) that they would expect from a guru or an Ashram.

Some of the people who read this book may be looking for a guru. Not surprisingly, they feel that someone, somewhere, might have some significant insights into the world that we all find so frustrating and confusing.

Clearly, some of the people who come to Jesus regard him as a guru, and want to test out whether he is worth listening to and following.

Just such a person was the individual we call the

'rich young ruler' in 10.17–22. 'Good Master' is what he calls Jesus – a typical address to a guru. And his concern is about what is worth doing and what is not worth doing. 'What good thing must I do to inherit eternal life?'

Clearly, he expected some wise and profound reply. But all that he got was a simple, almost insulting reply, repeating what he already knew. 'Keep the ten commandments'. Jesus interestingly misses out the first four commandments which relate to God, and gives him only the six which relate to fellow humans.

'All this I have done since I was young', he replies.

'One thing you lack', says Jesus. 'Go, and sell all you have, and give the proceeds away to the poor. Then come, and follow me.'

At this, the man's face falls. He has many possessions.

'How tough it is for rich people to get into the Kingdom of God', comments Jesus.

So what is the answer to someone seeking the truth, seeking the way, seeking the life worth living?

Jesus's answer is twofold. First, there is a base line of common human commitments which must not be violated. There are commitments of respect for other people's lives, loves, possessions and good name, and for one's own integrity and family (10.19). That is the first insight of Jesus. Following your own star must not be at someone else's cost.

But the second insight has to be set beside it. Following Jesus's star cannot but be at your own cost. If you look away from yourself, and look to Jesus, then the possibility of self-fulfilment becomes more remote. Self-renunciation replaces it.

So, elsewhere, Jesus sets out his 'wisdom', the things which as guru he tells his would-be disciples:

The one who wants to save their own life will lose it

But the one who loses their own life on behalf of me
and the gospel will save it. (8.35)

This is the great mystery that Jesus brings into the
world for all who seek a guru. It is the mystery that
self-seeking, even with the highest motives, leads
nowhere. The search for wisdom, insight, eternal life
has to be suspended so that the present need for
discipleship can be met.

And discipleship is costly. It is easier for a camel to
get through a needle's eye than for a rich person to get
into the kingdom of God, says Jesus (10.25).

Some people do it.

Peter declares, 'We have in fact left behind everything to follow you' (10.28). The reply of Jesus is clear:

There is not anyone who has left house, brothers,
sisters, mother, father, children or lands for my
sake and the gospel's

who will not receive in this present life a hundredfold
houses, brothers, sisters, mothers, children, and
lands, plus persecutions, plus eternal life in the
coming age. (10.29–30)

What Jesus means is this:

If you are up there looking for truth or wisdom or
beauty or eternal life, you will not find them. They will
elude you. People at the front turn out to be at the
back, whereas people at the end of the line turn out to
be at the front! (10.31) The mystery of this guru, Jesus,
is that personal searches have to be subverted by search
for the Kingdom:

Seek first the Kingdom of God, and his rightness,
And all these other things will be yours as well.
(Mt. 6.33)

Everything comes back to you, once you have made the total commitment. The degree to which you make a commitment will determine the degree to which you get the kingdom compensations – now and later.

If you ask, 'When and what do I receive?', there are some answers. You receive back again what you have given up – many times over. And you receive troubles, persecutions. And at the end, you receive your hopes and dreams – the Kingdom of God.

16: Master

In this situation, some people become disciples.

We usually say 'Get your head in the right place' or 'Get your heart in the right place.' Jesus does it all upside-down. Get your feet right first – 'follow me'.

Jesus never calls people to believe in him. Jesus never calls people to love him. Jesus calls people only to follow him.

If people did believe in him or love him, that was fine. But he as Master never asks for it. He asks for following discipleship.

1. Start with your feet. Jesus first of all calls people to follow him. Everything else is only necessary if you are following. So Simon and Andrew (1.16–18), James and John (1.19–20) and Levi (2.14) are called to leave their work and go after him. 'Following' Jesus becomes synonymous with 'being a disciple'. 'On the way' (8.27, 9.33, 10.52) means 'on Jesus's way, going with him'.

2. Then share your meals. Get your *stomach* in the right place! Jesus invites his disciples to share meals with him (2.13–17). It's a major element, as we see in the chapter on 'Parties in Houses'.

3. Then leave some things behind. House, brothers, sisters, mother, father, children and lands are named as things which disciples leave behind to follow (10.29). When the disciples go out on a mission, they are to have no evident possessions (6.8–9).

4. Then have things in common. Jesus used the boats of his disciples, probably (3.9, 4.1, 4.36, 5.18). He also used their homes (1.29,35), or perhaps his own house (2.1), and the house seemed fairly large (2.3–6). The disciples are told to 'stay wherever they will have you', on their mission (6.10). Money is shared among disciples, as is clear from Judas 'having the purse' (Jn. 13.29). The purpose is plain: the disciple group are to have as much as possible of their possessions and livelihood in common.

5. Then learn to share a common destiny. Despite constant complaints from disciples, Jesus keeps telling them of his impending suffering and death (8.31, 9.12, 9.31, 10.33). But he plainly expects them to share in the same destiny:

> The cup that I drink, you will drink.
> The baptism I get, you will get. (10.39)

And it is possible that Jesus thinks of 'giving his life as a ransom for others' (10.45) as something which the disciples also can enter into. The 'Son of Man' is not Jesus alone, but the clear destiny of humanity which is opened up by him, which now is continued by all who are with him and in him, who 'fill up' his sufferings (Colossians 1.24).

6. The heart and the head? There are plenty of misunderstandings. 'Who do you say I am?' (8.29) produces a confession that he is Messiah, but his Messiahship is immediately misunderstood. The disciples' misunderstanding is a continuing theme in Mark, right up to the end, when despite their protestations of loyalty (14.26–31) they all forsake him (14.50) and Peter denies him (14.66–72). The moral must be: Don't trust your head and your heart. The heart leads people astray! (Mt.15.19)

17: Blasphemer

Mark's Gospel opens with the announcement, 'The beginning of the Good News of Jesus, the Messiah, the Son of God' (1.1).

These two titles – Messiah, and Son of God – were the titles by which Jesus came to be known in the first century. The first, Messiah in Hebrew, Christ in Greek, was the title which those of Jewish background would use. The word *messias* simply means 'a person who had been anointed', and it was used to denote a number of persons in the Old Testament who had been 'anointed' for some special office, especially as a king, a priest or a prophet. In Jesus's day, people were expecting a leader to arise who would be 'God's anointed one', or God's Messiah. But there was widespread disagreement as to who or what the Messiah should be. The Dead Sea sect of Jesus's day even had two Messiahs – one of the House of David (a king) and one of the House of Aaron (a priest).

The second title, 'Son of God', would have been significant to non-Jews. For Jews, every faithful son of Israel was a 'son of God'. Every Israelite was a son of God by birthright, and could 'become' one by faithful obedience to the Law. So that Jesus would also have been a 'son of God' like any other Israelite.

But on non-Jewish, Gentile lips, 'Son of God' would inevitably mean 'one of the gods', or 'divine man' or 'a god in human form'. Mark's Gospel was addressed to people in Rome, many suggest, or at least to non-Jews outside Palestine. To them, the term 'Messiah' would be meaningless, but the term 'Son of God' would immediately communicate. So that it is entirely understandable when the Roman Centurion at the cross witnesses: 'Truly, this man was a (or the) Son of God' (15.39).

The two titles triumphantly come together in the high priest's question in 14.61: 'Are you the Christ, the Son of the Blessed?'. Moreover, the decisive and conclusive charge against Jesus in his trial was that he uttered blasphemy, that is, that he took the name of God in vain, or pretended to have the power of God, or took away from the glory of God.

> You have heard the blasphemy.
> What more evidence do we need? (14.64)

The variety of witnesses who could not agree among themselves (14.56) indicate the confusion that Jesus's teaching clearly caused. So, too, do the questions of 12.13–34, which were designed to trap Jesus in his teaching. The reason why they wished to trap him was, quite plainly, because the popular report made Jesus a radical and innovatory teacher. If only he could be persuaded into open and clear statements of blasphemy, then he could be condemned. The penalty for blasphemy was stoning to death (Lev. 24.16, I Kings 21.10), which was later meted out to Stephen (Acts 6.11; 7.58). But this was probably not in the Sanhedrin's power, hence they sent him to Pilate, once they had got the condemnation for blasphemy clear.

Blasphemy was something more than heresy. It was for proclaiming heresy that Paul was given the punishment of 'forty lashes save one' on five occasions (2 Cor. 11.24). But heresy was not what they wished to lay on Jesus. It was blasphemy that the reports accuse him of.

To the faithful Israelite, Jesus's activity was blasphemous. Indeed, according to Mark, Jesus acts not so much as a son of God, but acts as if he *was* God.

1. He forgave sins, which only God could do, and this is described explicitly by the scribes as blasphemy (2.7).

2. He ignored the Law when it suited him, and invited law-breakers and sinners – that is, he put himself up as a new 'definition' of God's law (2.17).

3. He acted as if he were someone greater than God who had given the Law, and let people rejoice in him as the Bridegroom (2.19).

4. He broke the Sabbath, and said it was made for humans, not for God (2.27). To offend the Sabbath was to blaspheme the God who caused it by 'resting' on the seventh day (Gen.2.1–3).

5. He claimed to be greater that the Prince of Devils, Beelzebub, which according to current belief only God was (3.22–7).

6. He taught that failing to discern the Holy Spirit as present in what he did, was itself blasphemy (3.29), and that he himself could declare that other blasphemies would be forgiven (3.28).

7. He taught that the Law of God was at odds with God's real purposes, which only God, presumably, could do (over defilement, 7.1–8, 14–23; honouring parents, 7.9–13; divorce, 10.2–12).

8. He claimed that his authority came from God – by implication, as he had no other source, and refused to admit any (11.27–33).

9. He was thought to have said that he would destroy the Temple (14.57–9), which was destroying the God of the Temple.

10. He admitted to being Messiah, Son of God (14.61–4), which was claiming to make himself almost equal to God (Jn.5.18; 10.33,36; 19.7), and to be 'Son of Man at the right hand of Power', that is, God (14.62).

What all this means is clear. On the one hand, contemporary religious leaders were justified in accusing him of blasphemy. On the other hand, Mark is saying to his Gentile readers: Yes, this man Jesus you can worship as God.

As I put it in *Secular Christ* (p. 89), 'Jesus goes about his business as if he were God Almighty'. 'Jesus is the secular activity of the hidden God'. 'Jesus takes over the activities normally performed by God, and does them himself'.

It is interesting that in Mark, Jesus only calls God 'father' on two occasions. In 13.32, 'only the Father' knows the day or hour of the end of all things. At 14.36, Jesus prays 'Abba, Father, all things are possible for you – Take this cup away from me'. There are, of course, many other places where God is implied or suggested. The amazing thing is that in a totally God-centred culture, the radicality of Jesus is allowed to appear even to the point of blasphemy.

From all the references, it is clear that Jesus is not a 'fundamentalist'. Fundamentalism is a way of interpreting the Old Testament as if it were the very words of God, absolutely correct and unquestionable. This attitude does not go back to Jesus's day. There are different ways of understanding scripture. In Mark, people come up and question Jesus about his attitude to various pieces of the Old Testament, and he feels perfectly free to set aside this or that tradition, as we have seen.

Yet, equally, Jesus is not a liberal. There were liberal rabbis, followers of Hillel, who generally 'lightened' the requirements of the Law. But in some cases, as with divorce, Jesus made the Law even 'heavier'.

Jesus's attitude was neither fundamentalist nor liberal, but radical.

18: Politician

A politician in today's language is someone who engages in organised activity concerning public life. A politician is an active participator in the processes of government. A politician takes seriously the decisions, the decision-making machinery and the decision-makers of the time.

In these senses, Jesus is a politician. He is not a political leader. He does not see the arena of political life as the one appropriate for the Kingdom. He does not set up or champion a political party or a political campaign. But this does not mean he is not a politician in the senses just indicated.

To start with, in order to do what we have so far said he does, he *has* to be a politician, otherwise he cannot have any effect on people living in his society. For his society is one in which total control is exercised by religious authorities, and this affects the whole of life.

Systematically, Jesus exposes this whole religious system. All the kinds of individuals whom the system excludes, Jesus brings in – a madman (1.23–7), a leper (1.40–2), a paralytic (2.1–12), publicans and sinners (2.15–17), law-breaking disciples (2.23–7), a man with a withered hand (3.1–5). No wonder:

> The Pharisees began plotting with the partisans of Herod, to see how they could make away with him (3.6)

Jesus predicts as much. Kingdom practice is totally

irreconcilable with the existing Judaistic system. You cannot put new wine into old wineskins (2.22).

But the social-political significance is vital. Madness, leprosy, paralysis, fear of disobeying the Law are all conditions which keep religions in business! Religions show you how to keep pure, and what to do if you are not pure. If the whole thing is broken down, then religion breaks down. And if religion breaks down, the religious authorities, such as the Pharisees, are redundant, and the political powers, the Herodians, are threatened. Temple sacrifices, observance of Laws and Sabbaths are all blasted away if Jesus, the Holy One, includes people without any of them!

Later, it is not just individuals whose healing secures a breaking of the system. It is the regulations and their assumptions themselves that are blasted away. One by one, the essential economic, political and ideological aspects of the system are dismantled: marriage and divorce (10.1–12), wealth (10.17–27), political power (10.41–45), the Temple (11.12–25; 12.1–12), imperial taxes (12.13–17), Jewish Law (12.28–35), scribal authority (12.38–40), Temple power (13.1–2). Israel, the fig-tree, is sterile (11.12–14, 20–4). The great questions can no longer be answered within its terms (11.27–33). The vineyard is to be given to others (12.1–11). No wonder they look for a way to arrest him (12.12).

Jesus's practice and project thus carry four strong negatives for the existing system:

1. Jesus denigrates openly and on specific occasions actually reduces the power of those who hold the upper hand – the rich (10.17–25), those in authority (10.42–4), the money-changers (11.15). 'Let children come to me instead', he says (10.13–16).

2. Jesus trivialises the issues which the politico-religious system magnifies. To the chief priests, scribes and elders, who demand to know by what authority he is acting, he only exposes the impossibility of simple

answers (11.27–33). To the Pharisees and Herodians, who want to trap him into opposing giving tribute to Caesar, he merely replies, 'Use Roman coins for the Romans, use temple coins for the temple' (12.13–17). To the Sadducees, objecting that resurrection implies polygamy, he replies that God is 'not the God of the dead, but of the living', and we can only know about the living! (12.18–27) To the scribe, checking him on Jewish orthodoxy about the two great commandments, he says, 'Great, but that's still not the Kingdom.' (12.28–34)

3. Jesus takes on the politico-religious system on its own terms, and exposes its falseness, presumption and ridiculous anti-human values. Hence the debates about the Sabbath, cleanliness and the Law. 'You watch out for scribes!' (12.38–40) he tells his followers. Even the chief priest (14.60–63) and Pilate (15.1–5) are made to look foolish. Faced with his powerlessness and potential, they can do nothing.

4. Jesus submits to the power of those whose power he denigrates. 'The Son of Man is delivered unto men, chief priests, scribes and elders' (8.31; 9.31; 10.32–4). Even the authorities he despises (12.33–40) he takes seriously (12.28–34). The Pharisees and Herodians (12.13–17) and the Sadduccees (12.18–27) are exposed on their own terms. Their power is at an end, even though they continue in power and are allowed to overcome him.

19: Counter-Politician

From the beginning we have seen how Jesus personally helps those victimised by the system, so that they are able to grab hold of some life for themselves. The lepers, blind, maimed, paralytic and law-breakers are restored. Restoration happens in three ways – first to themselves as full persons, second to their families as full members, third to Israel as participant members. And only when Israel refuses to receive them does the counter-community of the Kingdom have to replace the old Israel.

Jesus raises up the social and political weaklings – the poor, the little people, the servants and the children. His disciples still cannot see it. In response to a debate specifically on the nature and persons of power, he ridicules 'lording it over others', and demands that first people are the servants of all (10.35–45).

It all becomes clear when Jesus reaches Jerusalem. He enters the great city riding on an ass, 'a colt on which no-one has ridden before' (11.2). And his disciples proclaim 'blessings on the Kingdom of our father David, which is about to come' (11.10). No-one can be confused about the claim. It is a new reality, a new political set-up, a new system of everything that is being announced. And it can only be symbolised by a powerless, untrained, youthful animal, which could not overthrow anyone, except perhaps its rider!

The Kingdom of the powerless, the untrained, the youthful, conflicts hopelessly with the kingdom of the powerful, the sophisticated and the established. Hence, the cleansing of the temple (11.15–18), is designed to cast out the rich and the robbers who made money out of others' needs, and to re-establish the poor, the outsiders, and the Gentiles, for whom it had been intended and who are kept out by the money-changers who demand that Gentile money be changed for Temple money.

In its place, Jesus confirms his own Temple in humanity and his synagogue in the home. He demolishes religion's control over the after-life (12.18–27), overturns the Davidic supremacy (12.35–37), upholds the selfgiving of the poor above the stewardship of the rich (12.41–44), replaces the Temple (13.1–2), interprets the present and future Israel solely in terms of himself (13.3–37), has his own private anointing outside the Temple (14.3–9), arranges an alternative Passover (14.12–16) and institutes his substitute Passover, the Eucharist (14.17–25).

Thus Jesus the counter-politician draws up the lines of his alternative politics. First, he sets out his own stall – the ass, the cleansing, the anointing, the last supper. Second, he exposes the existing powers – the Temple, the Romans, the chief priests, the Pharisees, Herodians, Sadducees and scribes. Third, he sets up alternative objects as models – the child, the colt, the little ones, the anointing woman, the widow. Fourth, he sets up a place where these alternative political realities can be acted out and supported – the disciple group.

The relevance of Jesus's counter-politics is clear as soon as one recalls its contracts with normal politics, in his day and ours:

1. The political system of the Jewish authorities is based upon a divine legal code, administered by its accredited and often hereditary heads. For this, Jesus substitutes the outlines of a political state determined by human love and by the imitation of a divine 'father'.

A new political force of radical humanisation and secularisation is thus released into history.

2. The political system of the Romans is based upon dominance, paternalism and the power of force, administered by those whose loyalty is estimated upwards, but never downwards. For this, Jesus substitutes the germs of a new political state, determined by each being the servant of the other and of lordship existing in servanthood. A new force of radical egalitarianism and 'levelling' is thus released into history.

3. Political power is held by those who have social and economic power. The social and economic systems of Judaism and of Rome are based upon the possession of land, wealth and appointment. For this Jesus substitutes a realm in which the poor and the 'little ones' have the places of privilege. A new force of radical reversals is thus released into human history.

4. Political power is held within nations and within established elite groups. Judaism, Zealotism, Priesthood, Roman authority all exist by honour and lordship within carefully demarcated ethnic or power groups. For this Jesus substitutes those outside such groups. A new force of radical ecumenicity is thus released into history.

Thus, Jesus is a subversive. He subverts the politics of Jewish authority by setting up his own free society of equals. He subverts the politics of Rome by setting up mutual servanthood in a new society. He subverts the politics of personal power, wealth and possessions by making the small and poor the centre of the Kingdom. He subverts the politics of elites by opening the Kingdom to those on the frontiers.

And Jesus is also a community builder. The beginnings of a new system, the community of the disciples, disciples to the Kingdom, are set in motion. Everything that is needed for human life – society, politics, religion, sacredness, relationships – is now in the nascent community around himself. Within that small community Jesus works at developing a new world of relationships in which common family, common privations, common disciplines, common residence, common work and common cash are the rule. The alternative political reality is being built up, even while the old ones are still in control. Its first form is the disciple group. Its second form is the post-resurrection church.

20: Journey Downwards

Jesus is the classic case and the example of the middle class person who makes a conscious decision to come down in the world. From the middle class he opts for the poor.

We have a saying in Urban Theology Unit which I do not like but which I daily discover to be true: Where you are is who you are. That is, the physical, geographical and sociological *place* which a person occupies, in fact determines their personhood, their politics, and their theology. 'Who you are' simply cannot be divorced from the location you occupy in the world itself.

Assume that you are an affluent, educated, white, middle class, sophisticated Christian – and most of the readers of this book will be such, or at least inevitably moving in that direction. You cannot avoid being what you are. You cannot run away from what your birth, upbringing, education, church allegiance, reading habits, cultural interests, friends and peer-groups have made you. You are a rich person, not a poor person. You cannot deny who you are as a result of all the influences which have gone to make you up, and all the preconceptions and preoccupations which presently determine your attitudes. Nor yet should you try to deny who you are.

But you can do something. You can decide whether you are going to put yourself in a situation where all these tendencies and elements within your makeup are going to be confirmed, protected and exaggerated – or whether you are going to put yourself in a situation where these tendencies and elements are going to be questioned, exposed and curtailed.

Our experience in the Urban Theology Unit is that all of us desperately need this kind of re-education through re-location. Our experience is that no amount of courses on sociology, urbanology, contemporary problems, poverty, racism, educational deprivation, economic injustice or world issues in fact change people's perceptions, much less their commitments. But living alongside the poor, the manual workers, the underprivileged, the marginal, the one-parent families, the Asians, the West Indians, the unemployed teen-agers, the drop-outs and the left-behinds – that can change both perceptions and commitments. It is education at the bottom. I am at the bottom of my own experience as a person, reduced to basic simple experience alongside other diverse human beings. I am at the bottom in my learning processes, learning at the very basic levels of food, housing, personal habits, basic amenities maintenance, basic human relationships. I am at the bottom in vocational and career intentions, as someone with apparently many gifts to bestow on others, who has to discover what it is to receive gifts from those to whom I thought I had so much to give.

Only within this context have I been able to see 'conversion' taking place. 'Conversion' (*metanoia*) had always been a fascinating but confusing thing to me. Clearly, in the New Testament it meant 'a complete and radical about-turn of everything', 'a change of heart, soul, mind and body'. But I only began to *see* conversions actually taking place when I saw people actually changing their whole lifestyle, career prospects, conceptions of others and of things, use of money, personal habits of clothing, speech, use of time, interests, pre-occupations and friends – and doing all this *because* they placed themselves within an alternative Christian community within a basically alternative environment.

So I have to say to the church: if you want to have conversions to Jesus Christ, you must have places and communities dramatically different from the good typical church. The good typical church, I know, is not only affluent, middle class, educated and successful, but also often charitable, accepting, supportive, loving, tolerant, broad-minded, enlightened, conscientious and imaginative. The bad typical inner city church lacks many of these – it is poor, working or non-working class, uneducated, and a failure. And it often is mean, narrow, isolating, vicious, unloving, intolerant, narrow-minded, unenlightened, not very conscientious or imaginative!

But it is in such contexts and with such people that I have learned what 'liberation' is – the kind of liberation I and people like me need, the kind of liberation Jesus got for himself. By turning his back on the scribes and their knowledge of the Law, in which he had been schooling himself, he suddenly discovers a new kind of law going on among the poor. By ignoring his own background and family support group, he suddenly finds the love that is latent in the unloved and unloving, the outcasts and the law-breakers. By moving out from a synagogue-centred ministry, out into houses and out into the open city he suddenly finds that the agenda of survival and significance among 'the common people' are more relevant than those of the closed religious circle.

The journey downwards is not a model for everyone. When I spoke about it to black theological students in South Africa, they said, 'This is not for us. We have been kept down. Now we are on a journey upwards.' So, let us emphasise two things again.

Every gospel model is not a model for everyone. It is a model for those for whom it is intended. And those for whom it is intended are those for whom other gospel elements have already raised some questions. The journey downwards is for people who are doing well, who have raised themselves, who have acquired things, or people, or education, or money, or status. Jesus called them the rich, 'those who have'.

The Kingdom is now. And if the Kingdom is now, then the Kingdom reversals are taking place, and things that seem valuable are rejected. And already, here and now, there is the community of the Kingdom, the representative heads of the new twelve tribes, the people of the alternative messiah. And they are *already* being hailed as 'holy', 'happy', blessed'. Kingdom realities are already let loose, and available to all who will not exclude themselves from them by holding on to the rags and tatters of money, success, acceptance and education.

So, the question is, *'From what can I come down?'* Where have I landed myself on a plateau which excludes me from the Kingdom down there in the ghetto? How have I lifted myself above the lot of the world's eighty per cent? Where have I, a minority world person, taken to myself what could have been shared with majority world people? Where have I, a privileged minority in the minority world, excluded myself from the majority around me?

To Other Jesuses

There seem to be different Jesuses.

So peddle me if you can your whole Christ,

Your Christian presence in all things,
Your Christ of glory,
Your Christ prayed to –
  by nations and prime ministers,
  by archbishops, and bishops,
  by serious responsible economists,
  by boards of believing investors. . . .

For all I know, it could be right.
It could be the true Christ.
Or some legitimate contemporary version of the true
  Christ.

But I must settle for what bits I know –
And have the courage to stand by them,
So that it can be
As determinative, liberating and empowering
For me where I am,
As the other pictures are
For you, where you are.
My bit does not exclude all you can know.
It does not exclude the Christ
Who stands with the powerful, the successful,
  the ebullient, the confident, the balanced,
  the suburban, the educated, the fulfilled.

But I can only stand beside
The Christ I know.
And that Christ I know
Stands hesitantly on the edge of reality,
Pushed and pulled by the hordes of people,
Held on to, tenuously but desperately,
  by people moving in paper boats into a storm of
    juggernauts,
  by youngsters with pop-music cassettes,
    sitting before judges, assessors, examination
      boards,
    responsible newspapers, parental expectations,

the future of the world,
(and me, of course, half with all of them),
    plucking a leaf to live by,
    a word to hold on to,
    a way to open up to,
    from a reality
    twenty centuries waiting his constant rebirth
    at the hands of history's nobodies.

To You, Radical Jesus

A Radical goes to the roots,
Finds out the base of things,
Lives by the original source
Cuts out additions, revisions, rationalisations,
Goes back to the basic beginnings.

You were not a Revolutionary.
A Revolutionary seeks achievable changes
After which all will be well.
You were a Radical.
A Radical seeks continual change
Because everything will never be right.
The Revolutionary works for
One great heave to overthrow the status quo.
The Radical persistently revolutionises everything.

You were not a Liberal,
A Revisionist, or an Enlightener.
You were a Radical.
A Radical does not trust
The evolutionary processes of humanism,
The discoveries of science and technology,

The mutual manipulation of sociological theories,
Personal growth, self-fulfilment, self-enrichment,
  'experiences',
Radicals know themselves too well
To trust any of them.

You were not a Fundamentalist,
a Bible-worshipper, a Literalist.
You were a Radical.
You went to the roots of everything,
Simply, without prevarication,
Demanding that basic human laws be respected and
  held to –
    like the word of one person to another,
    like the commitment of a woman and a man,
    like the rest after labour that bodies need,
Whether the old Law said it or not.

Jesus, you were a Radical.
You pointed away from yourself
To a reality and a situation to which you were
  obedient.
You called it 'God's Kingdom', 'God's Rule'.
A Radical Reality in which there could be now
  equality between all people,
  raising up of everyone's gifts,
  significance within the secular,
  forgiveness for the offender.

Jesus, you proclaimed a new radicalism needed by
  the new Kingdom.
A radicalism of total commitment
to that which was sure, though invisible for everyone,
  though few knew it, for all time, though especially
  now.

Part Four: Radical Movement

John said to Jesus:

'Teacher, we saw someone casting out demons in your Name. But he was not a follower along with us. So we stopped him, because he was not following with us.'

And Jesus said:

'Don't stop him. There is not one who does a mighty deed in my Name who can quickly speak against me.

'Whoever is not against us is for us.

'Remember: Anyone who gives you a cup of water
                because you are of the Messiah's
                movement
                I can certainly say to you
                will not lose their reward.'

Mark 9.38–41

21: A Long Shot?

This book is an attempt to do one simple thing: get myself and others to face up to the radicality of Jesus, and to indicate one or two ways in which that radicality is needed today.

I am aware that a vast stretch of Christianity exists between you and me and those first followers. There are many other things said by some of those followers, in the New Testament and elsewhere. It is true that the Radical Jesus I describe jumps out of Mark's Gospel rather than the others. Luke's Jesus is more like a humanitarian counsellor, Matthew's like a community lawyer, John's like a philosophical debater. And Paul, though he knows more than anyone what radical obedience means, invents (he says by revelation) a new kind of Christianity. Yet the lines of Jesus's radicality are never totally erased. Luke even tells the Acts of the Apostles as if they are a re-run of the acts of Jesus in his Gospel.

The doctrines that result from Jesus are often a problem. Some of us cannot take them all – not because they are not true, but because they have been used to shield people from following the radical Jesus. If it's the radical Jesus whom people want to call 'Very God of Very God', or 'King of Kings and Lord of Lords', then that's great! But so often it is some triumphalist Christ who is quite the opposite of the Jesus we have seen. Or, if it's trusting oneself to the Radical Jesus that people mean when they insist that we are 'saved by faith alone', then that's fine. But so often it is faith in some kind of transaction, or some kind of personal experience which they mean, and that is something else.

I do in fact know that I stand with all the Christians in all times in wanting to say that this Jesus is the Decisive One, for God and humanity. Beyond that, we do well not to quarrel with what we cannot say, each of us, but rather concentrate on what we can say, and even more, what we can *do*. Go for the things which are for you, not for the things which are not for you. We all follow, of necessity, half in darkness. But follow where you see the light, and for the rest let others follow where they see the light.

It is inevitable, too, that one should not be content with simply following the Radical Jesus, but desire and attempt to set down a whole theology based on it. I myself want to do it – perhaps a 'Radical Dogmatics' one day – why not? Yet I do not want even to hint at it here. If people find themselves demanding to know how major theological questions about salvation, resurrection, christology and eternity fit in with this book, then they could hunt out a copy of *Secular Christ*. The first chapters are on Mark's Gospel from a 'secular' point of view. But the last hundred pages attempt such mysteries.

And now, in the last Part, I want to try to help myself and the reader to try to put some kind of life together, in the light of the Radical Jesus, and to try to say what that might mean in terms of attitudes and commitments today.

And to do that is not easy.

Contemporary Christians have got to make a long journey backwards before we can be entitled to be called the company of Jesus. We must go back behind the alliances of western powers which established a form of religion called Christianity as the religion 'by law established' in Western European states. We must go back behind the wars of the twentieth century when we made God bless guns, tanks, armies and nuclear missiles. We must go back behind the 'Christian' invasion of Africa, of India, of North America, of Asia.

We must go back behind the 'Manifest Destiny' which made white Christians all but obliterate the American Indian. We must go back behind the churches imposed on workers by industrialist dictators and child employers. We must go back behind the devoted Christian traders who hauled six million black people into slavery across the Atlantic, killing another six million *en route*, singing hymns to Jesus at the same time. We must go back behind the building of great cathedrals in Britain and Europe by serf labour, victimisation and oppression. We must go back behind the Holy Roman Empire, the Constantinian peace between Christ and state, behind the obedience of early Christians to secular rulers. We must even go back behind Paul in Romans 13, with his 'powers that be are ordained by God'.

We must go back to the Jubilee of Jesus, the Kingdom of God, the liberation of all people by the Son of Man; back to Jesus the radical, which is what this whole book is about.

I know there was a time when I did it differently.

I know there was a time, at least for myself personally, when with apparently impartial search, I was able to sit down and open the books about the Gospels, or the New Testament, or theology, or ethics, or truth or reality. To do so was, I thought, the way in to being a Christian, even a theologian. Now it seems to me that those things can scandalously block the way to being a Christian or a theologian.

Now, I cannot allow the story to be hijacked any more by students, academics, study groups or denominations, twisting it all to suit their already conceived positions and commitments. No, the world needs the

Radical Jesus. We all need the stories of Jesus as a legitimation and empowerment for the faintly held but desperately needed hunches, conversions and total changes which they open up. We need Jesus, not as part of the structures by which we control and are controlled by our environment – but as part of the nagging, persistent call to be, and be supported as, something radically different. Now we need Jesus, not as someone in whom we believe, for whom we make claims, and around whom we create stances, but as someone who might believe in parts of us.

So, this Jesus is someone whose faith-actions provoke mine. His walking on the water is not a wonder to be gaped at, but a provocation and invitation for me. His raising the dead is not a sign of his divinity but a call to mine. His casting out devils is not God's magic but our mission strategy.

And as for all the books, I find the study of the Gospels opening up in a totally new way once I see them, not as records to be debated so that I get it right in my head, but as living dynamics and actions to be entered into, even imitated, that I get it right in my feet and hands!

Of course, this is all very problematic and dangerous. It is a very terrifying thing to raise these radical questions. I only do so at all because as a disciple of Jesus, I am compelled to, especially as a 'minister of religion', when Jesus blasted away religion in favour of the Kingdom!

22: Taking Pages from Jesus's Book

1. Jesus represents new possibilities for people.
Jesus invariably brings something novel into situations.
Jesus provides ways for a person to move, to change, to discover, to revolutionise.
Jesus shows how people can be used.

This means that we have to provide 'ways of escape',
that we have to point people to different methods and directions,
that we dig holes for people to fall into, prepare support mechanisms for failure,
that I am free to be used by others.

2. Jesus shares himself with others, is person-oriented.
Jesus seeks out individuals, involves himself in individual situations.
Jesus goes to the people and deals with them one by one.

This means that we are to give ourselves to people,
that we have to seek out those who need and who need the most,
that we are not disciples to ideas, or beliefs or principles,
that I am free to give myself in an attitude of love.

3. Jesus goes to the poor and the outcast.

Jesus feasts with groups or individuals who are excluded from normal society.

Jesus forms a movement of the poor.

Jesus holds up the happiness of the poor as judgement and mercy for all.

This means that the disenfranchised or neglected are our special concern,

that outsiders need to claim Jesus and the Kingdom in their own way,

that the poor are the people of God's special care,

that I must learn to be poor.

4. Jesus heals people before he preaches to them. He satisfies human and bodily needs first.

This means that community needs have to be met first,

that the city writes the agenda,

that the poor and needy and sick have the priority,

that I am 'saved' by the life of Jesus, not by anything else.

5. Jesus acts out some contrary actions that are, and become, significant.

Jesus does things which create stories, or which create surprises.

Jesus suggests that gestures, actions, events are more important than words.

This means that we are to act out, symbolize, embody a new liberated existence,

that we are to engage in actions in which others may join,

that deeds become the unwritten book that others read,

that I must put my mouth where my actions are – or keep quiet.

6. Jesus creates and uses groups relevant to particular things.

Jesus has a group of women engaged in ministry with him.

Jesus utilises homes, and the groups there – Lazarus, Mary and Martha.

Jesus utilises the tax-gatherers' grape-vine and works through it.

This means that not everyone is right for everything at every moment,

that we have to work through structures and groupings that work,

that kingdom-gatherings do not have to be only church congregations,

that I am most useful with people like myself.

7. Jesus goes for people who are active, or prepared to act.

Jesus calls people in the midst of their jobs – fishermen, tax-collectors.

Jesus wants people who have shown that they are capable of doing something!

Jesus picks people who are on the go, already busy. He does not pick the idle.

This means that the Kingdom needs workers, not shirkers,

that talents and abilities are able to be identified and used,

that secular capabilities are sometimes useful,

that I can and must act.

8. Jesus calls individuals to discipleship.

Jesus gets hold of people without heavy conceptions or head-trips.

Jesus acts so as to free up others also to act.

This means   that we are called to be apprentices, lear-
ners, understudies, stand-ins to Jesus,

that we are marching to a secret drum,
Jesus's,

that we must expect people to hear
personal calls and be ready to support
them,

that I can expect the Radical Jesus story
to call me also.

9. Jesus gets a group to do things together.

Jesus is leader to his followers and supporters.

Jesus spends time on creating a nuclear group.

This means   that we have to sense what is there so as
to bring people together,

that we have to spend time with the
disciple group, or create one,

that I must be a disciple alongside others.

10. Jesus uses powerlessness.

Jesus avoids taking positions of power or influence.

Jesus has no office, or status, or position, or honour.

Jesus holds up the poor as those to whom the Kingdom
is given.

This means   that we can choose or adopt powerlessness,

that positions of non-power are significant,

that oppression is everywhere a possibility,

that I must learn to be powerless.

11. Jesus disciplines himself.

Jesus has a baptism to face, and is straitened until it is
done.

Jesus disciplines himself to God's Kingdom, to embody
and serve it.

Jesus has no place to lay his head, denies himself.

This means   that the joy of obedience comes with
discipline,

that there is a proper asceticism in
discipleship,
that I am safest when I am without
security.

12. Jesus is willing to be a failure, to die.
Jesus is powerless, prepared to be overcome, to be
crucified.
Jesus gives his life a ransom for many.
This means that Jesus's disciples are called to give up
life, called to give themselves vicariously
for others,
that disciples are thrown into situations
and have to take whatever comes,
that disciples are powerless but free – free
from having to succeed,
that I may be rejected and fail.

23: Searching in the City

Radical Jesus has always had a genius for taking his best people and throwing them into the worst places.

It is so today. Many Christians, would-be Christians and fellow-travellers are looking for alternatives. They are looking for something worthwhile and challenging to do. Some of them come with their search to the inner cities.

The Churches that are still there are often in a pathetic shape, and can do little to help them – except by (hopefully!) welcoming them. The recent Church of England Report, *Faith in the City* (Church House Publishing, 1985) shows exactly the tragedy and the need.

But there are also Christian disciples there, and Christian congregations. Often it is easier to encounter radical Jesus followers there than elsewhere. Many stories are in Colin Marchant, *Signs in the City* (Hodder Paperbacks, 1985), which also lists twelve pages of 'Signposts' – with addresses. Three of my own books tell other stories (see chapter 27).

In my experience, many people looking for new orientations for Christian discipleship need help and stimulation during their search. It was to provide such that we started the Urban Theology Unit in 1970. UTU is an association of Christians from all denominations who are committed to the search for relevant Christian discipleship in the city. We work through our members in many places, sharing their gifts, insights, commitments and experiments. We have our main base in

Sheffield, in two large old houses in a pleasant inner city street, and in the homes of a strong supportive community in the neighbourhood.

We are a 'community of study and commitment' which shares a simple lifestyle, eats, worships and relaxes together, and seeks to be used in local churches and community projects, often within the Sheffield Inner City Ecumenical Mission, of which UTU is a member. We have serviced a small, part-time, ecumenical staff. The place and style are unpretentious, homely and modest.

Recently, we produced a new prospectus to cover our work for the next few years. It was a long, collegial process, deciding what to say. Finally, we listed 'Our Methods' as:

Listening to the groaning and travailing of the city,
Sharing skills and experience and learning communally,
Learning with pioneers who work alongside poor and disadvantaged people,
Provoking and supporting each other honestly, critically and creatively,
Helping people to face unpleasant realities and take risks,
Renewing ourselves and each other in places where life is draining,
Searching with others for new vocations and ways of being disciples,
Exploring new personal and corporate styles of Doing Theology,
Supporting people in struggling situations, small churches and alternative communities,
Being grasped in fresh ways by Jesus and the Gospel,
Raiding the Christian storehouse to offer fresh tools and ingredients,
Existing by faith, in smallness and simplicity,

Encouraging the transformation of society by being irritants, models and catalysts.

All this in practice means a variety of Courses and Consultations, ranging from the 'Study Year' from September to June to two-year weekend courses or single three-day events. Ministers and lay people, women and men, are roughly equal in number, from all denominations and none, of all ages and academic and non-academic backgrounds. We'd love to send you a prospectus and invite you to come and see us. Write to me at Urban Theology Unit, 210 Abbeyfield Road, Sheffield S4 7AZ.

24: Joining a Committed Group

If you want to be committed to the radical Jesus, you will probably need a wider community of like-minded disciples. There are hundreds of different sorts of communities, groups and organisations in Britain today. Some of them are residential, most of them have residential centres plus wider memberships and activities. There is a *Directory of Christian Groups, Communities and Networks* available from the National Association of Christian Communities and Networks, Westhill College, Selly Oak, Birmingham B29 6LL.

The Community which I find supportive and challenging is the Ashram Community. It began with a few of us in 1967. We now have around 80 members and many more sympathisers in many parts of the country.

Every now and then we invite each other to make our witness to what the Community is. In a recent issue of our Journal, *ACT*, called *What is the Ashram Community?* everyone had a go at it. This was my contribution:

The Ashram Community is a community of disciples of Jesus Christ which seeks to provoke new calls from the Gospel, enable new ventures of faith, support new enterprises in service, experiment with new ways of action, have as much as possible in common, pioneer new action in politics, discover and stand beside those in need, provide alternative models for the churches.

Each year, all members covenant themselves to the Community by signing the membership form and committing themselves for the ensuing year. The Membership Commitment is as follows:

The Ashram Community seeks to be a community of disciples of Jesus of Nazareth. Our lifestyle experiments are attempts to embody the spirit, life and teaching of Jesus today. We are committed to supporting each other in ways in which the inspiration of Jesus takes us; and to sharing and celebrating together the sufferings and joys of those ways.

We see ourselves as a Christian community, a gathering of individuals and congregations. We regard ourselves as a part of the Church. We are open to all, whether committed Christians or not.

Membership of the Ashram Community is open to all who desire to commit themselves to the Community and its life.

Corporately, we commit ourselves to be a Christian community of care to each other and to the world.

Personally, we commit ourselves to a search for a meaningful personal faith, vocation and lifestyle.

In practice, this means that we commit ourselves to:

1. Attend whenever possible the two annual Community Weekends in Spring and Autumn.
2. Share in local groups, community houses, congregations, projects or other activities whenever possible.

3. Make an annual financial commitment both to support Ashram Community and also to give to wider needs.

Our current local community commitments include a variety of projects, all differing ways in which members in different contexts respond to the Gospel. These at present are:

A house and community service project in Spark-brook, Birmingham,

Several autonomous community houses where members and others live together,

A yearly day's pay project for a specific need outside Britain,

A members' income sharing project,

A community shop/workshops/centre/residence project in Sheffield.

Radical Jesus campaigns based on town centre shops,

Pilgrimages, holidays, community visits.

News of all these is contained in a bi-monthly newsletter, *Act Together*, and in our journal, *ACT*. Enquiries to Community Office, Ashram Community, 239 Abbeyfield Road, Sheffield S4 7AW.

25: Eucharist of the Radical Christ

Parts are indicated for: A Leader, a Reader, two Groups (two sides of the congregation) and All.

1. Call to Celebrate

Leader: Let us celebrate the good news of Jesus.

Reader: The Spirit of the Lord is upon me. She has anointed me to preach Good News to the poor. She has sent me to proclaim release to the captives, and recovery of sight to the blind, to set free the oppressed, to proclaim the year when the Lord will save his people.
(*Luke 4.18–19*)

All: The acceptable year is upon us!
The liberation of God is in our midst!
Let us celebrate the Kingdom.

2. A Song
(*Any traditional, modern or specially written song*)

3. The Reading
(*The Reader reads the Gospel as chosen*)

4. Creed of the Radical Christ
(*Read responsively in two groups*)

Leader: Let us declare our trust in Christ
All: I trust myself to Jesus Christ;

Son of a carpenter	Calling God Father;
One with his people	Creating a new family;
Draining the old wine	Fermenting the new;
Open to everyone	Narrowing the gate;
Deliverer of captives	Binding the free;
Bringer of peace	Stirring up strife;
Creator of unity	Dividing asunder;
Hope for the hopeless	Destroying our hopes;
Crucified for all	Compelling cross-bearers;
Emptying the tomb	Going ahead of us.

All: I trust myself through this Jesus
To the Kingdom he points to,
To the Father behind it,
In the Spirit who sustains it,
With disciples everywhere who live for it.

5. Peace and Offertory

Leader: Let there be living
All: Let there be sharing of living
Leader: Let there be liberation to live
All: Let there be living to liberate.
       (*All stand, join hands in a circle, and say*:)
       We are the Body of Christ.
       We were all baptised into one Spirit.
       Therefore let us pursue all that is good,
       and trust in his Way.
Leader: The gifts of God for the people of God!
All: We, though we are many, are a single loaf, a single body;
       For we all have a share in this bread and wine.

6. Eucharistic Prayer

Leader: We act again the meal of Jesus with his disciples.

All: Jesus, while he was being betrayed,
Gave thanks for bread.
He took a piece, and broke it, and said:
My body is broken for you.
Share this among yourselves, and remember me.
He also passed a cup, saying:
My blood is poured out for you, that you may live.
Share it and rejoice.

Reader: We give thanks for our common life,

All: For its brokenness

Reader: For the presence of Christ in our struggle.

All: For the promise of freedom to the powerless,

Reader: For the privilege of sharing.

All: For the coming of Christ again and again.
(*A period of silence or spoken thanksgivings*)

7. The Sharing

Leader: Now let us take this bread, break it, and share it in the name of Christ. (*Leader breaks the bread.*)
Let us also take this wine, being poured out for us, and drink it in the name of Christ. (*Leader pours out the wine.*
The bread and wine are passed round with the words '**The Body of Christ**' *and* '**The Lifeblood of Christ**', *with the response* '**Amen**'.)

Leader: It is the mystery of ourselves that we have received.

All: The Spirit of the Lord is upon us. She has anointed us to preach Good News to the poor. She has sent us to proclaim release to the captives, and recovery of sight to the blind, to set free the oppressed, to proclaim the year when the Lord will save his people.

8. Intercessions

(*Concerns and requests for prayer are made by all present.*
***A Liturgy of Prayer**, which follows below, can also be used here.*)

9. Close

Leader: The grace of the Lord Jesus be always with us.

All: The grace of the Lord Jesus, and the love of God and the fellowship of the Holy Spirit be with us all, evermore. Amen.

Urban Theology Unit

26: Jesus Pattern Prayers

A Liturgy of Prayer
(Read in turn, or the Leader introduces short periods of silence by reading the headings.)

1. Jesus and his Disciples are Dependent

Verse: Jesus says to us, 'Take only what you need'.

For others: Lord, we pray for those who are dependent on others for food and shelter.

For ourselves: Lord, in affluent society, burdened with too many possessions, help us to live your year of jubilee.

2. Jesus and his Disciples are Marked People

Verse: Jesus has no form or comeliness, that we should notice him, and no beauty that we should desire him.
He is despised and rejected.

For others: Lord, we pray for the ugly and disfigured in mind and body, that in them we might see you.

For ourselves: Lord, give us the ability to love the unlovely; and to become signs of contradiction for your Kingdom.

3. Jesus and his Disciples are Powerless

Verse: Jesus says, 'I send you out as lambs in the midst of wolves.'

For others: Lord, we pray for all who struggle for power to change their lives; and for those in power, that they may have their eyes opened to the needs of others.

For
ourselves: Lord, train us to be powerless.

4. Jesus and his Disciples are Carefree

Verse: Jesus says, 'Give no thought for tomorrow'.

For others: Lord, in a world where you're nobody unless you're going somewhere, we pray for the wanderers who are going nowhere.

For
ourselves: Lord, liberate us from the cares of the world, the deceit of riches and the pride of life.

5. Jesus and his Disciples are Misunderstood

Verse: Jesus says, 'You have the secret of the Kingdom.'

For others: Lord, we pray for those who cause horror, ridicule and laughter, because they struggle against the stream, in a society where to be different is to be misunderstood.

For
ourselves: Lord, help us to understand why we do what we do – object to things, seem to know better, look for alternatives.

6. Jesus and his Disciples are Homeless

Verse: Jesus says, 'The Son of Man has no place to lay his head.'

For others: Lord, we pray for those for whom four walls and a roof are an unattainable luxury.

For
ourselves: Lord, we pray that we may stop building barns and storing up treasures.

7. Jesus and his Disciples Share

Verse: Jesus says, 'Love one another as I have loved you.'

For others: Lord, we pray for those who do not have enough to make them possessive, who have so little, yet share it.

113

For ourselves:	Lord, give us the will to have things in common.
Leader:	Jesus says, 'Those who have ears to hear, let them hear.'
All:	We have ears to hear, let us hear.'

Urban Theology Unit

A Commitment
(*To be said together*)

We commit ourselves
to hold to the truth as it is in Jesus,
to support each other in good and ill,
to challenge evil with the power of love,
to offer the kingdom in political and economic witness,
to work for the new community of all humanity,
and to risk ourselves in a lifestyle of sharing.

Sheffield Eucharist Congregation

A Benediction
(*To be said together*)

Hands of Jesus, bless us,
Arms of Jesus, uphold us,
Feet of Jesus, lead us,
Heart of Jesus, burn in us,
Presence of Jesus, be in our neighbour.

Ashram Community

114

27: A Guide to Further Reading

This is the second time in my life that I have tried to write a book about the one to whom I try to be a disciple. It is a funny feeling – to keep stumbling on new pieces of the mystery, as I have in writing this book, and to see it all happening still, just as he said.

My first attempt at a contemporary interpretation of Jesus was in *Secular Christ* (Lutterworth Press, 1968). The chapters on Christology, Ministry, Parables, Discipleship, Resurrection and Salvation in many ways supplement the present book. What I then heard as 'secular' is what now needs to be heard as 'radical', twenty years later.

Not all lives of Jesus put it exactly as I have done in this book. Obviously, liberal, revolutionary, fundamentalist, and denominational interpretations abound. The following are writers who follow lines similar to my own, though no one would agree with everything I have written.

Three thorough but fascinating books are good as guides to the situation of Palestine in the time of Jesus: Joachim Jeremias, *Jerusalem in the Time of Jesus* (SCM Press, 1969); J. D. M. Derrett, *Jesus's Audience* (Darton, Longman and Todd, 1973); and Geza Vermès, *Jesus the Jew* (Fontana, 1978). A good technical introduction to the intricacies of the study of the Gospels is W. Barnes Tatum, *In Quest of Jesus: A Guidebook* (SCM Press, 1983). In the present book, I have, of course, simply told the story as Mark tells it, without raising questions of historicity or relations with other Gospels.

Our interpretation of Jesus as a Radical can be taken further in a number of recent books which, although they take very different lines from me, yet give the same general picture, or support special aspects of it. I name three. Adolf Holl, *Jesus in Bad Company* (Collins 1972) shows Jesus as a 'criminal', homeless, celibate, and an associate of the poor and outcasts. Albert Nolan, *Jesus Before Christianity* (Darton, Longman and Todd, 1977) traces 'the Gospel of Liberation' back to Jesus's work among the poor and his confrontation with the powers. Leonardo Boff, *Jesus Christ Liberator* (Orbis Books, 1978) studies the whole question of 'Christology', and relates Jesus as Liberator to other views in a most striking way.

At a fairly popular level, several recent books open up the radicalism of parts of the Gospel story. Donald B. Kraybill, *The Upside Down Kingdom* (Marshalls, 1985) is a beautifully constructed and striking volume on Jesus's teaching on the Kingdom of God. Christopher J. Sugden, *Radical Discipleship* (Marshalls 1983) surveys all the Gospel passages on discipleship and sees them as a clear call to contemporary commitment. A larger study is Thaddée Matura, *Gospel Radicalism: The Hard Sayings of Jesus* (Gill & Macmillan, 1984).

The methods of contemporary Bible study and contemporary identifications or 'snaps' with the material are expounded in John D. Davies and John J. Vincent, *Mark at Work* (Bible Reading Fellowship, 1986). Other books on Mark's Gospel and its interpretation today are referred to there also.

Readers who wish to pursue an inner city sense of identification with the Gospel story of Jesus can do so in three recent books by myself. *Starting All Over Again* (World Council of Churches, 1981) has 'hints of Jesus in the city', with Jesus as loner, deviant, bondman, juggler, politician and Pied Piper. *Into the City* (Epworth Press, 1982) tells the Sheffield Inner City Ecumenical Mission story in terms of incarnation, healing, parables, acted parables, etc. *OK, Let's Be Methodists* (Epworth Press, 1984) sees John Wesley fulfilling Jesus's claim in Lk.4.18, 'as it is fulfilled in every true minister of Christ,' and inaugurating a mission of and for the poor.

One inconvenient oddity to Christian radicals is that the word 'radical' is often used in the press to describe people whose views are 'extreme'. Thus we hear of 'radicals' applied equally to fundamentalists and to liberals. And even to Tories!

Bishop David Jenkins is a case in point. His views have been consistently 'liberal' for twenty years, as his books indicate. But as soon as he expresses scepticism about the Virgin Birth or the Resurrection as physical occurrences, he is called a 'radical'. Hence, when John Stott writes a 'response to current scepticism in the Church' and calls it *The Authentic Jesus* (Marshalls 1985), the Bishop's views are regarded as 'radical'.

Whereas, if David Jenkins is to be called a 'radical' it should be because of radical convictions about Jesus and the Kingdom, such as in this book – or about liberation theology, which he has recently welcomed.

Indeed, a British Liberation Theology may well be a way for an authentic grass-roots Jesus radicalism to be expressed in the future. So far, the signs are small. However, I am now the convenor of a *British Liberation Theology Project* under the auspices of Christian Organisations for Social Political and Economic Change (COSPEC).

The Urban Theology Unit has many publications which might interest those who wish to take further contemporary urban mission and radical discipleship.

Please write to Urban Theology Unit, 210 Abbeyfield Road, Sheffield S4 7AZ.

The three publications produced for the Radical Jesus Campaigns make useful small booklets for group work. These are: *Radical Jesus Manifesto* (Ashram Community), Edward S. Kessler, *Radical Jesus in Parables* (UTU) and *Radical Jesus Workbook* (Ashram Community). £1.70 post free from Ashram Community, 239 Abbeyfield Road, Sheffield S4 7AW, for all three.

Your Movement Needs Me

Jesus, I want to commit myself to your community –
A community of Sisters and Brothers,
   upholding each other,
    giving their gifts and possessions to each other,
    exposing each other's weaknesses in love,
    provoking each other to deeds together.

Jesus, I want to commit myself to your Movement—
a Movement for
   the raising up of the low,
   the feeding of the hungry,
   the liberation of the captives,
   the seeing of the blinded,
   the hearing of the deafened,
   the freeing of the slaves,
   the unbinding of the burdened.

To this end, your people find themselves involved up
   to the hilt in politics –

Not just primarily the politics of parties or slogans or
  political leaders,
Whom they often expose
As Jesus did,
  (and as we might do, demanding Tories, SDPs,
  Liberals and Labour heed people other than their
  commitments).

But submitted to the Politics
  of embodying a better way,
  by common wealth,
  by common work,
  by common life.

Such politics can appear
  in demonstrating against injustice,
    (like cleansing the Temple);
  in proclaiming the power of weakness,
    (like entering the city on an ass);
  in exposing the authorities,
    (like challenging Pilate);
  in denying the stated issues,
    (like the debates about who is great);
  in unmasking established financial monopolies,
    (like the coin as Caesar's or the Temple's).

Such politics begin with commitment,
  commitment to victimised people,
  commitment to radical change,
  commitment to pioneering projects,
  commitment to new communities,
  commitment to ultimate values.

Which means joining
  the peace movement,
  the movements for social justice
    equality of sexes,
    equality of races,
  the movements towards common wealth,

        common futures,
        common destinies.

But also joining with each other and others,
    in pioneering new political alliances,
        of the poor,
        of the disenfranchised,
        of the non-technological
        of the post-industrial,
        of the nutty pioneers of a new world.

Such politics has the hope of success, because it is
    not in any party programme, because it endlessly
    provokes
        new actions,
        new commitments,
        new experiments,
        new soldarities,
        new policies.

This is the Movement, let's join it.
These are the People, let's find them.
This is the Truth, let's act it.

Notes

It is impossible to give the 'scholarly' justification for all the interpretations in this book. But the following are a few 'lines' which readers might like to follow up.

Note on Gospel Translations. There are, I believe, many connections between Jesus's situation in AD 30–33, the situation of the early Church in AD 50–65, and the situation in the Church for which Mark was written (assuming it is Rome) in AD 66–70. See my article, 'Mission in Mark' in *New Testament and Missiology*, ed. John Ferguson (International Association of Mission Studies, forthcoming).

Chapter 2. For Mark's construction of 1.1–15 as a way of 're-doing' the exodus and wilderness experience and settlement in Canaan, see John Drury, 'Mark 1.1–15: An Interpretation', in *Alternative Approaches to New Testament Study*, ed. A. E. Harvey (SPCK, 1985).

Chapter 8. Possibly the 'crowd' always means the poor and outcast. See Ahn Byung Mu, 'Jesus and the Minjung in the Gospel of Mark', in *Evangelism and the Poor*, ed. V. Samuel & C. Sugden (Oxford Centre for Mission Studies, 1983).

Chapter 10. For the replacement of synagogue by house in Mark, see Elizabeth Struthers Malbon, 'His own house: Mark 2.15 in context', in *New Testament Studies*, April 1985, pp. 282–292.

Chapter 11. For lively interpretations on this theme, see Rachel Conrad Wahlberg, *Jesus According to a Woman* (Paulist Press, 1975). For much detail and contemporary background, see Ben Witherington, *Women in the Ministry of Jesus* (Cambridge University Press, 1984). For parallels and comparisons in the stories of Jairus and his daughter and the haemorrhaging woman in 5.21–43, see John Davies and John Vincent, *Mark at Work* (Bible Reading Fellowship, 1986) ch. 13.

Chapter 12. The interpretation of the feeding of the 5,000 in 6.31–44 as a would-be political rising is in Davies and Vincent, *Mark at Work*, ch. 14.

Chapter 16. For the idea of ransom as being in line with the self-sacrificial death of the Maccabbean *Eleazar* in c. 160BC (IV Maccabees 6.24–30 and 17.20–22), see C. K. Barrett, 'The Background of Mark 10.45', in *N. T. Essays in memory of T. W. Manson* (Manchester University Press, 1959).

Biblical References

Then and Now

Study Questions for group and individual use

Part One: Radical Jesus

Chapter 1. (a) How have your origins restricted you? (b) How far away are you from where you started?

Chapter 2. (a) What effects did Jesus's life until thirty have? (b) Who today are 'sinners' in the Gospel sense (p.16)?

Chapter 3. (a) Find examples of 'levelling' in the New Testament. (b). What are sonship and wilderness in your experience?

Chapter 4. (a) How do Galilean/inner-city backgrounds affect discipleship? (b) In what other contexts would Jesus be at home?

Part Two: Radical Kingdom

Chapter 5. (a) Who are the sick, converts, outcasts and officials in your town? (b) How would such people respond to Jesus? Or how do they?

Chapter 6. (a) 'Jesus implies that people who wish to change must find areas, commitments, groups, actions which require and expect them to behave differently'. List some possibilities. (b) What is your Manifesto as a disciple? How does it compare with Jesus'?

Chapter 7. (a) How do you understand the fact that Jesus has to be waylaid to get him to heal? Is healing his chief work as liberator? (b) How can modern disciples call forth the faith potential within people needing healing today?

Chapter 8. (a) Do you think demon possession is happening today? (b) What demons are being cast out so that people live by their own power? (See last paragraph)

Chapter 9. (a) How do Jesus's journeys downward – first to common people, then to the lowest people – provide a model for us? (b) List ways in which today's poor are 'sinned-against'.

Chapter 10. (a) 'Mealtimes demonstrate his radicality'. How can ours? (b) 'The house replaces the synagogue'. Should it replace church buildings?

Chapter 11. (a) Women's needs, actions, ministries and rights are affirmed by Jesus, while privileged claims (his mother's) are denied. What does this suggest for today? (b) Is the 'equality and partnership of women' clear in your church?

Chapter 12. (a) What is the 'struggle' for whose success Jesus works? (b) How is 'being handed over', rather than defending himself, 'success'?

Chapter 13. (a) Jesus's ministry to foreigners challenges all exclusiveness. Who are our foreigners? (b) What does Mark 13 say to 'frightened, excluded, marginalised, dispossessed' Christians today?

Part Three: Radical Destiny

Chapter 14. (a) What five things are most important to you? What does Jesus say about them? (b) Is Jesus always 'the classic Alternative', different, perverse?

Chapter 15. (a) How are you 'saving' or 'losing' your life? (b) 'Personal searches have to be subverted by search for the Kingdom'. What could this mean?

Chapter 16. (a) Obeying the Master involves

following, eating, leaving behind, having things in common, sharing destiny, and then bringing heart and head. Where are you up to? (b) How can we share Jesus's cup and baptism?

Chapter 17. (a) Is the Radical Jesus 'blasphemous' for main-line Christians today? (b) Jesus was 'neither fundamentalist nor liberal, but radical'. Do you agree?

Chapter 18. (a) What religious systems and practices in our churches does Jesus 'blast away'? (b) How can we express Jesus's 'four strong negatives for the existing system' in political action?

Chapter 19. (a) What might the four lines of Jesus's alternative politics lead us into today? (b) How can the new 'community of the disciples' work within society as it is?

Chapter 20. (a) How can you make a Journey Downwards? (b) 'Conversions to Jesus Christ' require 'places and communities radically different from the good, typical church'. Examples?

Part Four: Radical Movement

These chapters suggest basic ingredients for being in Jesus's Movement – a Different Christianity (21), a New Lifestyle (22), Ways of learning (23), a Community (24), a Communion Sharing (25), Jesus-centred prayers (26), and relevant books (27).

The questions for each chapter are simply: (a) Which of these is for me, now? (b) Who can I find to take it further with me?